Finding My Family

By David Holmer

PublishAmerica
Baltimore

First printing

This publication contains the opinions and ideas of its author. Author intends to offer information of a general nature. Any reliance on the information herein is at the reader's own discretion.

The author and publisher specifically disclaim all responsibility for any liability, loss, or right, personal or otherwise, which is incurred as a consequence, directly or indirectly, of the use and application of any contents of this book. They further make no representations or warranties with respect to the accuracy or completeness of the contents of this work and specifically disclaim all warranties including without limitation any implied warranty of fitness for a particular purpose. Any recommendations are made without any guarantee on the part of the author or the publisher.

PublishAmerica has allowed this work to remain exactly as the author intended, verbatim, without editorial input.

Hardcover 978-1-4560-7835-5
Softcover 978-1-4560-7834-8
PUBLISHED BY PUBLISHAMERICA, LLLP
www.publishamerica.com
Baltimore

Printed in the United States of America

Dedication

In loving memory of...
Eugene W Huskey (1929-1982)
Frances E Huskey (1924-2007)
Kenneth E Clark Sr (1931-1990)
Joan G Clark (1931-2003)
Kenneth E Clark Jr (1952-1994)
LaDonna L Clark (1967-1984)
Susan E Loring (1950-2009)
Steven C Lancaster (1951-1978)
Ronald C Hoard (1953-1984)
Theodore J Clark (1928-1993)
Robert C Ridge (1948-2006)
Karen L Waldron (1951-1993)

Special thanks to:

Donna Holmer, for all the hours of proofreading and re-proofreading.

Wanda Bouchikas, for all the times spent going to cemeteries together and sharing an interest in genealogy.

Bob Bouchikas, for adding adventure like a spontaneous Blue Angel show... twice!

Shirley Kloko, for her encouragement and opening up all her records for me.

Randy and Dick Kloko, for their exhaustive research both foreign and domestic!

Norma Daniel and **LaDonna Sells**, for their early work on our Cross ancestry.

Chris Boger, for working side by side throughout the years (despite of all that bragging about your family having two published genealogy books).

Sheri Hoard, for continually reminding me where Uncle Ron and Uncle Steve's graves are.

Amber Story, for last minute proof-reading and grammar checking.

And, to anyone else that I may have forgotten, who ever had to stop and let me check out a cemetery!

Table of Contents

Introduction

The history of genealogy can be traced back to the beginning of civilization, starting with the Sumerian King List. Other examples of family lists can also be found in religious texts. For example, the Holy Bible actually contains three lists of genealogical information in Genesis 5, Genesis 10 and Matthew 1. This information can be used to settle issues of authority and succession. For example: if you are related to a current monarchy, your lineage can tell you where you are in succession to the throne!

Over the past year, genealogy has become more prominant in mainstream America with four television shows: "Who Do You Think You Are?" (NBC), "Find My Family" (ABC), "Faces of America with Henry Louis Gates Jr." (PBS) and "Generations Project" (BYU). In the news, genealogy has also become more prominant with the 2010 U.S. Federal Census' campaign "Portrait of America". This exposure has helped people become more aware of the excitment that comes from uncovering the stories about a person's family history. I have had this same experience whenever I uncover a new piece of my family history; and, this excitment builds upon itself.

I decided to send away for the marriage license of a John Holmer that listed the bride as Anna, even though my great-great grandmother was Emilia. I still remember the excitement that I felt as I opened the letter to discover that the full name of the bride was Anna Emilia Anderson! When I searched for the church that was listed as their place of marriage, I became even more excited discovering that it was still standing and that they were one of its founding members! But, nothing can describe how I felt the first time I was standing right in front of it, looking at it with my own eyes.

The excitment grew even more when the door was opened and I was invited in to see inside the sanctuary. I saw the craftsmanship that went into the Swedish structure and the original pipe organ. The place was perfectly preserved for over 125 years, including the hand-painted wall behind the altar. Even more exciting was when I returned the very next day for their Sunday worship service and partook in communion, kneeling in the very spot and in front of the same congregation as my family ancestors! Excitment like this is very hard to keep to oneself.

As I would tell my stories about all the exciting things that I was finding out about my family history, people constantly wanted to know more. Eventually, I realized that what people wanted to actually hear was the details in how I was making progress with my research so that they could discover their own exciting family history. As I helped people begin their own research into their family histories, I also realized that I had developed a pattern over the years that has been proven to be quite effective for the most productive and accurate research.

Finding My Family is simple to use and easy to get started. My book provides clear and concise directions on how to maximize the results of your genealogical research. I have accumulated ten years of experience in researching genealogy and have seen my techniques work where others have failed. I know it can work for you!

David Holmer

How to Use This Book

This Book Is For You

- If you are interested in finding your ancestors.
- If you are beginning your family tree.
- If you are frustrated with genealogy tips telling you WHAT to do, but leaving out the more important HOW to do it.
- If genealogy is overwhelming to you.
- If you are confused with record accuracy.
- If you have generation gaps in your family history.
- If you want fresh new ideas for your research.

How This Book Can Help You

I have organized this book from the point of view of one who has never researched genealogy before and likes to read and understand a concept while trying it out. Each chapter takes you further into genealogy with step-by-step instructions and examples, multiple examples given as appendices, and footnotes. However, you may prefer to skip the first section and get to the advanced part of the book for generation gaps or fresh new ideas in researching. You can always come back to the first section, which includes the basics.

The following is a brief synopsis of each section of the book. This will help <u>you</u> decide the best way to begin finding <u>your</u> family.

Part I

Chapters 1 through 7 take you on a simplified journey to understanding how to find your ancestors and begin your family genealogy. These chapters deal with how to interview and begin with name gathering, locating graves, gathering birth years and years of death, and how to use this information to go through census records and gather exact locations of families. You will also find out what makes each census unique, adding personal touches to your research.

Although you may gain some dates from interviewing alone, the information you get from tombstones in Chapter 3 is more reliable. Chapters 4 will aid you for going through the US Census and finding locations. From these locations, you can use Chapter 5 as another source for accurate and more complete dates. The most personable information can be gained through newspaper articles and keepsakes discussed in Chapters 6 and 7.

Part II

Chapter 8 offers definitions and descriptions of forms that are standard throughout genealogy. Chapters 9 and 10 give you more help and resource information for intermediate researching of other records and troubleshooting common trouble areas. Chapter 11 and Appendices show you the various options available for compiling, recording and publishing your research.

Chapter 1
"My Journey into Genealogy"

City College of San Francisco

I was first introduced to genealogy by my biology professor, who gave our class an assignment: To fill out our family trees as accurately as possible. The Family Tree is an ideal goal, being small enough for any beginner to start. The assignment gave me specific goals to work towards in genealogy. It set a priority on what type of information I was searching for, such as, focusing on births, marriages and deaths more than on education, military service or occupations. It also set a priority on parents, grandparents, and great-grandparents more than on aunts, uncles, great-aunts, great-uncles and cousins. From this assignment, I became interested in finding my family.

Helpful Tip # 1 Write a Mission Statement

A Mission Statement, like an assignment, is a specific task, written out with definite goals. Much of my success was due to keeping focused on the assignment instead of letting myself become too distracted. Having a written mission statement also helps to keep you from becoming overwhelmed with genealogy records and record keeping!

Genealogical Research

When I received the assignment, I started filling out my family tree with what I already knew. I called my relatives and found out what information they knew. From this oral history, my genealogical research had begun. Being away at college, the next step in my research was basically limited to just using the internet.

Surnames are the basis for most online databases, guides and other genealogy projects. Internet search engines are a quick way to research family information like census and vital records. When the surname was so uncommon that it produced very little results, I used the Soundex option, which includes alternate names and spellings, to produce more results. I also used these resources to trace my family surnames and find their origins, Coat of Arms or, sometimes, original meanings.

Helpful Tip # 2 Keep a List of Surnames

A List of Surnames is an excellent reference tool to help improve your search engine results. I used my list to record all surnames, alternate names, name changes and alternate spellings that I have come across in my research. I was able to expand my research gathering because I recorded all naming information in a list of surnames. (For an example, see Appendix A: List of Surnames.)

Trouble-shooting and Problem Solving

When I searched the internet, I started running into obstacles and problems that I was having trouble dealing with. I tried to use the tips that are online, but they were not explicit enough to help me. I had a long list of what to do, but no explanation for how to actually do the research. Sometimes, I would get stuck in a "run around" going from one website of links to another website of links and couldn't find any solutions for my problems. I started keeping track of all the websites that I had visited.

Helpful Tip # 3 Keep a Works Cited Page

A Works Cited Page is simply a list that gives credit to the resources where you found your research information. I used my page to quickly find good sources that I have used previously and to identify wrong or inaccurate information from poor sources. I benefited both ways because I recorded all my resources in a Works Cited page! (For an example, see Appendix B: Works Cited.)

I soon realized that the internet was not a very good place for someone like me to start their genealogical research. I looked forward to Thanksgiving and winter breaks so that I could actually do some other types of research, like visiting cemeteries and interviewing family members. When I finally did get a chance to interview family members, I started running into other obstacles and problems. I realized that memories and family stories, although interesting, are not very reliable; however, a good interview can lead you to the perfect place for beginner's to start their research: the cemetery.

Results, Results, Results!

After visiting the cemetery, I started having success for getting results in my research. I had a greater understanding of what I was actually looking for in censuses and other records. Whenever I would come across a new cemetery, it always opened the door to some of the answers to problems that I was facing and even more possible leads. Eventually, I figured out the best ways of how to do the research to produce the most results. I even learned simple ways to record information so that I would not have to re-visit cemeteries that I had already been to.

Helpful Tip # 4 Carry a Notebook

Carrying a notebook has been very handy at times. I have used it for recording interviews, documenting cemeteries, and making age charts for easier census research. I have also used it to write down ideas and good resources that other genealogists have suggested. All information that I have is retained in a notebook.

Chapter 2
"How To Get Started"

The Privacy Gap

For most people, the right to privacy is a sacred trust that we hold dear to our hearts. What we share with others is very personal, especially if it is something about our family and loved ones. We use this special information to identify who we are. We believe so strongly in this concept that many countries have some type of privacy laws or legislation to help protect us. As we embark on this great journey of discovery, we meet our first obstacle that I like to call 'The Privacy Gap', a period of time from approximately the past 75 years to the present day.

During this period, most records are sealed from the general public. This generally includes any attempts for search and discovery or any rights for inspection of records, as well as, attempting to use, publish or disclose any personal information of another living person. These types of privacy legislation also differ between countries and change continuosly with amendments, executive orders, and written opinion of the courts. (There are even state privacy laws within these countries that also differ and change, similarly.)

To bridge this gap, we need to rely on oral histories to help us get back to where we can have full access to records. Depending on your age and the current year, you may need to go back somewhere between three to four generations:

```
    (First Generation)
 1  You

    (Second Generation)
 2  Your Father
 3  Your Mother

    (Third Generation)
 4  Your Father's Father
 5  Your Father's Mother
 6  Your Mother's Father
 7  Your Mother's Mother
```

Helpful Tip # 5 Start with What You Know

Start by making an ancestor (ascending) chart like the one above, filling in the names of everyone that you already know the names for. Be sure to use a pencil so that you can easily erase it and make changes to it later. If you do not know their names, write something like "grandpa's father" in their name space. If you are unsure about their name, write down what you think it might be with a question mark next to it. You can even write clues, like "adopted", to help you later in your search.

For Example, I knew that my paternal grandfather was Albert Holmer; that he was born on March 25; and that he came from Chicago, Illinois. I remembered that my paternal grandmother, Rhama DuBrill, passed away in 1976; that she had been married once before to a man named 'Huskey'; and that she also came from Chicago. I also knew that my maternal grandmother was Doris Kloko; and, my maternal grandfather was William Reed Jr, who passed away a long time ago. So, my chart looked something like this:

```
    (Third Generation)
 4  Albert Holmer
 5  Rhama DuBrill (?-1976)
 6  William Reed Jr (?-1960s or before?)
 7  Doris Kloko

    (Fourth Generation)
 8  Albert Holmer's father
 9  Albert Holmer's mother
10  Rhama DuBrill's father
11  Rhama DuBrill's mother
12  William Reed Sr
13  William Reed Jr's mother
14  Doris Kloko's father
15  Doris Kloko's mother
```

Informal Interviews

There are basically two ways to ask relatives for information. The quickest way is by an informal interview, which could be done through a telephone call or an e-mail. Be sure to keep your chart in front of you to refer to for where it is that you need help filling it out and to get you back on track in case the interview turns for a few minutes into polite everyday conversation. If they are unsure about exact names, ballpark is close enough. Remember, it is more important to just get something to start with.

For example, I found out that William Reed Jr was born in 1926 and died in 1951 from a motorcycle accident. His mother, Josie Reed, died in 1998 in Fort Myers, Florida, and was buried in Silverbrook cemetery in Niles, Michigan. William Reed Sr preceeded her in death. Also, I found out that Doris Kloko was born in 1932, died in 1995, and was buried near her house. Her mother, Bernice Bowersox, and her father, Ervin Kloko, were both buried in Silverbrook. And, her grandparents were Allen and Orpha Bowersox and Herman and Minnie Kloko.(1)

In another interview, I found out that Albert Holmer was born in 1919. His mother, Helen Becht, was buried in Watervliet cemetery. His father, Walter Holmer, remarried to another Helen, who was a school teacher in Gary, Indiana. Also, I found out that Rhama DuBrill was born in 1910. Her mother, Myrtle Mann, was buried in the Coloma cemetery. Her father, Allen DuBrill, died when she was around seven years old.(2) Now, my chart looked like this:

```
     (Fourth Generation)
 8  Walter Holmer (buried: Gary, IN ?)
 9  Helen Becht (buried: Watervliet, MI)
10  Allen DuBrill (?-1917)
11  Myrtle Mann (buried: Coloma, MI)
12  William Reed Sr (?-bef1998)
13  Josie Reed (?-1998)(buried: Niles, MI)
14  Ervin Kloko (buried: Niles, MI)
15  Bernice Bowersox (buried: Niles, MI)

     (Fifth Generation)
28  Herman Kloko
29  Minnie Kloko
30  Allen Bowersox
31  Orpha Bowersox
```

Helpful Tip # 6 Be Specific in Informal Interviews

When contacting relatives, be sure to be as specific as you can about what type of information you need. (For example, "Do you know grandma's maiden name?") Do NOT ask open-ended questions during this type of interview, which could overwhelm you with dates and places of everyone in your family from your siblings to shirt-tail cousins, getting you no closer to bridging the gap. Focusing your questions specifically to the third and fourth generations can completely fill in your chart usually in less than 12 minutes!

The Formal Interview

The second method of asking relatives for information is by a formal interview. There are quite a few differences between informal and formal interviews. Informal ones are usually between acquaintenances, very short, unplanned, focused with specific goals in mind, and controlled by the interviewer. Formal interviews are usually the direct opposite. The interviewee should be in control of the conversation. If needed, the interviewer can help by asking an open-ended question. (But, you want the other person to talk!) This type of an interview needs to be planned in advance and can easily go for a couple of hours. And, it is also usually with a stranger, which is why there is proper etiquette to be followed.

Etiquette changes slightly depending on the person to whom you would like to interview. Mainly, there are two types of individuals that you should be interested in interviewing: the family's oldest living relative(s) and the family's historian(s). However, if you are not familiarly acquainted with the person you want to interview, the very first step is to have the person who referred them give a courtesy call. (For example, if grandpa told you that his aunt, whom you have never met before, is the family historian on his side of the family, proper ettiquette is for you to ask grandpa to call her and explain who you are and that you would like to speak with her about the family.)

The Family Historian

There is usually someone in the family who is considered the family historian or family genealogist, who accumulates and organizes the genealogical information. When you contact them, be sure to give them the surname(s) of the family you are interested in learning about and schedule your visit in a week or so, giving them time to prepare. You may also want to prepare yourself by organizing your materials and making a list of which ancestors you still need names for.

During your visit, pay close attention to their collection of documents. Instead of asking for a copy of their documents, find out where and how they obtained them. (Remember the adage: Give a man a fish and he eats for a day, Teach a man to fish and he eats for a lifetime!) Be sure to write down the name of the newspaper(s) for all clippings. Also, be sure to ask about where relatives are buried, the name and directions to the cemetery and the general location of the graves within the cemetery.

The Oldest Living Relative

Our elderly relatives hold such invaluable information, and it is all volatile if we don't get a chance to listen to their stories and write them down. And, they actually want to tell us their stories and have us pass them down from generation to generation. Some times, genealogy can seem cold with hard facts and dates. Visiting the elderly and hearing their stories gives you much more personable information, which often offers clues about where you can start your research. Older relatives can also be very helpful in putting together and filling in what you have already started.

Helpful Tip # 7 Record Your Visit

Recording the interview allows your relative to go at their own pace and, at the same time, allows you to give them your undivided attention. However, it is important to ask for permission to record them when scheduling your visit.

This gives them time to think about it. Meanwhile, prepare yourself ahead of time by making sure your equipment works and that you have enough tape and batteries in case your visit runs longer than expected. Also, be prepared with paper and pencils in case your relative is hessitant or declines to be recorded!

One of the easiest activities to do to help jog a memory is sorting through the family pictures together. Photographs can contain all kinds of genealogical information from either the labeling of it on the backside or in the picture itself on the front. Older relatives can often identify faces in old photographs and tell you the story of what may be happening in it. It is also a good idea to go through pictures with them to help label them for future refernce and retain the most accurate information about the photograph.

Helpful Tip # 8 Take Along a Camera

Take a camera with you to take pictures of their pictures. It is important to have adequate lighting and set the original photo at an angle to refract any light from glossy finishes from hitting the camera lens. Prepare yourself ahead of time by making sure the camera works and that you have good batteries. Be sure and write down the picture number with the names to identify the faces in the photograph.

Chapter 3
"Paying Your Respects"

Visiting Cemeteries

Visiting a family cemetery can add invaluable information to your research from what is on the gravestone markers, including: full names, birth and death dates, and information about marriage, military service, and/or religious affiliations. You can also judge the impact your ancestor has had on the community and others from any epitaphs, phrases and/or symbols. When planning to visit a cemetery, keep in mind that cemeteries can be open or closed to the public and owned privately, by the city or township, by the state and/or by the federal government. You need to be sure and have permission or authorization to visit any privately owned or publicly closed cemeteries.

Helpful Tip # 9 Stop in at the Office

It seems that every time I stop into a cemetery office, I walk out with something more than what I had expected to find. Besides the usual exact location of graves, I have been surprised with a brochure with plats from readable stones done twice by the local Genealogical and Historical Society, a pamphlet with a cemetery plot map including names of the purchasers, and leaflets containing: the cemetery history, rules and regulations for debris removal, hours of operation and contact information.

Locating Graves

Graves are arranged into groups of eight called lots. Each lot has a top half and a bottom half with four graves in each. Some lots, when purchased together, are called family lots with an additional four small markers placed in each of the four corners and a large family stone placed in the center of the lot. Sometimes, a family will erect a mausoleum on their lot. Lots are arranged into groups called blocks. Groups of blocks make up a section. Sections of the cemetery are different areas or subdivisions that are assigned an alphabetical letter (A,B,C...) or a name. (For example, "Old" and "New" or "Garden of the Good Shepherd" and "Garden of the Last Supper") When you know the exact location of a grave, you find it by going in order from section to block to lot to grave.

When you do not know the exact location of a grave, you can usually find it by what I call a scanning pattern. I pick one corner of the cemetery to start at. I divide the cemetery into manageable areas using the cemetery roads and maintenance "alleys" (rows kept clear for water lines, etc.). I briskly walk up and down each rows in an area, reading the surnames off of each of the gravestones. I skip the stones that are unreadable because it takes too much time to successfully decipher them. However, I do stop to remove debris, like overgrowth, from hindering the grave's surname. I repeat this pattern for each area of the cemetery until I have found the grave that I was looking for.

Helpful Tip # 10 Talk to the Maintenance

The maintenance crew in a cemetery can be very helpful. Sometimes, their garage houses old records, file cards or other information on graves, from unmarked to exact location. Workers can be helpful with surnames and grave locations based on the various areas they've worked. Experienced workers might be able to tell you about landscape changes from tree removals to tombstone repositioning, burying an erect tombstone on its side and making it flush with the lawn for easier maintenance. I have saved time, located graves and even found information on the unmarked grave of an ancestor from talking to cemetery maintenance crews.

Cleaning Graves

Cleaning tombstones should be done by relatives and lot owners ONLY because it can easily cause irreparable damage. Wire or hard bristled brushes and abrasives will cause scratching and flaking. Cleaning ingredients will cause discoloring and leave a hazed coating. Pressure washers will erode, deteriorate and strip stones making them unreadable. However, family members can clean tombstones with two acceptably safe items used for limestone, sandstone, marble and granite tombstones: water and soft, natural bristled brushes. However, cleaning still needs to be very gentle and only on stones in a good, stable condition. Bronze tombtones, on the other hand, require minimal cleaning because they are coated with a sealant.

Helpful Tip # 11 Make a Cleaning Kit

One of the most useful things for my genealogy research is my tombstone cleaning kit. I start with a plastic bag, which serves as both the kit's container and as a means for debris removal. My kit includes: a bottle of water, which can be used and refilled for washing and rinsing the tombstone; a toothbrush, which can be used for brushing and light scrubbing of the tombstone; a small gardening spade, which can be used for lawn trimming around the tombstone; and, gloves. Making a cleaning kit can be as simple as these five items, but putting one together can give you a tool that you will use over and over again!

There are basically five steps to cleaning a grave. The first step is to expose the tombstone by using gloves and removing all lawn overgrowth. Tombstones that lay flat at lawn level are more susceptible to overgrowth, eventually covering the entire headstone with sod. The second step is to use a gardening spade and remove 2" of sod from around the tombstone. This will help prevent future overgrowths. The third step is to remove dust and dirt by sweeping stone with a natural bristled brush. The fourth step is to use water with the brush and remove any fungus and bird droppings by gently scrubbing in a circular motion. Rinse with water. The fifth step is to dispose of sod and overgrowth according to the cemetery's rules and regulations or by placing debris in a plastic bag to take home with you.

Documenting Your Visit

The oldest technique for documenting gravestones are chalk rubbings, the bulky, lifesize reproductions that eventually become smeared and messy. Another disadvantage of rubbings is their difficulty to make, requiring good stones that are NOT rough, eroded or damaged. In addition, most cemeteries and cemetery associations do not allow stone rubbings because they are a threat to stones, defacing them with color, seperation and flaking of the face. Today, there are many other better alternatives for both the researcher and the preservation of the stones.

Helpful Tip # 12 Go on Rainy or Cloudy Days

The weather can have a huge impact on a day at the cemetery. Sunny days are very difficult to document by using a camera. Light refraction or glares from the sun can shine on a lens ruining the picture; as well as, shadows from the photographer and trees can create sharp contrasts which also ruins the picture. Cloudy days are optimum weather conditions for photography by eliminating refraction, glares, and shadows. Rainy days are good for locating a grave, making them easier to read, and for cleaning.

Tombstone transcriptions, another simple alternative, are block form sketches. The rectangular, block-like form is always used, although the actual gravestone may be square, oblong or even rounded. When transcriptions are made digitally, they are still kept simple with plain text, using only letters, numbers and punctuation (no symbols or fancy font styles). Despite omitting the images and symbols, it is important to maintain all phrases, epitaphs and punctuation EXACTLY as it appears on the marker. Unreadable information must be put in brackets, even if the transcriber knows how it had read in the past.

For Example, my grandma and grandpa Holmer's gravestone is a double marker, rectangular in shape. It has flowers adorning both sides of the stone. Across the top, in large, bold lettering is our surname, Holmer; and, below it are two boxes with my grandma's information on the left and my grandpa's information on the right.(3) Making a transcription of their tombstone, I need to omit the flowers and boxes and put the information in block form so that it ends up looking something like this:

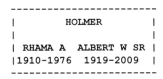

```
------------------------
|        HOLMER        |
|                      |
| RHAMA A   ALBERT W SR |
|1910-1976  1919-2009  |
------------------------
```

For more examples, see Appendix C : Tombstone Transcriptions.

Remember

Don't forget to update your ancestor chart, filling in dates from tombstones and any new names that you might have come across from visiting family plots. After visiting cemeteries, my chart looked something like this:

```
    (Third Generation)
 4  Albert W Holmer (1919-2009)
 5  Rhama A DuBrill (1910-1976)
 6  William Reed Jr (1926-1951)
 7  Doris A Kloko (1931-1995)

    (Fourth Generation)
 8  Walter Holmer (buried: Gary, IN ?)
 9  Helen Szczesniak (1897-1968)
10  Allen DuBrill (?-1917)
11  Myrtle A Cross (1884-1951)
12  William Reed (1897-1976)
13  Josephine Reed (1906-1998)
14  Ervin L Kloko (1899-1949)
15  Bernice Bowersox (1902-1957)

    (Fifth Generation)
28  Herman Kloko
29  Minnie Kloko
30  Allen Bowersox
31  Orpha Bowersox
```

Chapter 4
"Going Through Census Records"

United States Census Records

Starting in 1790, the United States began a federal census which originally numbered the whites, males by age, and slaves in each household. The format for these censuses changed drastically in 1850, when they started recording the names of every person in each household. These censuses have since been recorded every ten years. Records are then made available during the 72nd year after the census was taken. For example, the 1940 census will soon become available in 2012.

Censuses record the location of families at specific periods in time. Although these records are unreliable for name spellings and dates, they are very accurate as to the exact location of a family. They are even more useful when you can track a family's migration through multiple censuses, narrowing future searches of resources and knowing exactly where to look for these resources. To begin going through census records, it is easier to group them into four main periods of time (1790-1840, 1850-1880, 1890 and 1900-1930).

Names/Ages in	1900	1910	1920	1930
Surname,				
Father	#	#	#	#
Mother	#	#	#	#
Child	#	#	#	#

Helpful Tip # 13 Make an Age Chart

Start by making an age chart like the one above, filling in the names and ages from the information in your ancestor chart. If you cannot calculate their age, place a question mark (?) in the space. Also, use a dash (-) for years before birth and an "X" for years after death. A space between families makes it easier to read. For example, my age chart looked something like this:

```
Holmer,
  Walter      ?       ?       ?       ?
  Helen       3       13      23      33
  Albert      -       --      1       11

DuBrill,
  Allen       ?       ?       X       X
  Myrtle      16      26      36      46
  Rhama       --      mo.     10      20

Reed,
  William     16      26      36      46
  Josephine   --      4       14      24
  William Jr  --      -       --      4

Kloko,
  Herman      ?       ?       ?       ?
  Minnie      ?       ?       ?       ?
  Ervin       1       11      21      31

Bowersox,
  Allen       ?       ?       ?       ?
  Orpha       ?       ?       ?       ?
  Bernice     -       8       18      28
```

Online Census Indexes

The quickest and easiest way to search through census records is by using an online index, which is offered through websites by a paid subscription or as a free service. One disadvantage of free index services is that they usually contain only a few select census records. Another disadvantage is that they are often difficult to navigate as their record collection increases in size. There are even some free indexes that are advertisements and linked to paid subscription sites. Although these websites charge for access to census records, they are easier to navigate AND contain more complete indexes to census records.

Ancestry.com

For the beginner, Ancestry.com offers a wealth of FREE information to entice them into becoming paid subscribers. Some census indexes and previews are better than others. Typical search results list only name [with alternate spellings], County and State of Census (which is exactly what we should be looking for), and an estimated year of birth (which is how we can identify the family).

To search the 1930 Census Index, scroll over the "Search Tab" at the top of Ancestry.com's homepage (www.ancestry. com). From the drop-down menu, click on the link: "Census & Voter Lists". Find the section, "Narrow By Category", by scrolling to the right side of the page and click on the link: "US Federal Census Collection". Find the section, "Included Data Collections", by scrolling to the bottom of the page and click on the link: "1930 United States Federal Census".

On the search form, under "Name", fill in "Last Name" only! Next, under "Family Member", choose "Father" and fill in "First Name" only! Also, left-click on "Add family member", choose "Mother" and fill in "First Name" only! Again, left-click on "Add family member", choose "Spouse" and fill in "First Name" only using *both* first names separated by a space (father mother). Left-click on "Add family member", choose "Sibling" and fill in "First Name" only with child's name. Finally, <u>click</u> the SEARCH button at the bottom of the form.

For example, under "Name", I filled in "Last Name" with: Holmer. Next, under "Family Member", I chose "Father" and filled in "First Name" with: Walter. Also, I added "Mother" and filled in "First Name" with: Helen. Again, I added "Spouse" and filled in "First Name" with: Walter Helen. I added "Sibling" and filled in "First Name" with: Albert. Finally, I clicked the SEARCH button and found 10,714 matches sorted by revelance. Scrolling through the matches, I found only 1 match that had both Walter and Helen as spouses: (4)

```
View     Helen    Walter    city    abt
Record   Holmer             DuPage 1904
                            Illinois
```

If you scroll over View Record, you will get the census preview:

```
Name:          Helen Holmer
Age:           26
Estimated      abt 1904
birth year:
Spouse's       Walter Holmer
name:
```

Comparing the preview to my age chart, the difference between the ages of both Helens is seven years. Usually, the age differs by only 2-3 years. This, combined with the fact that there were no "Albert Holmer" in the search results for this preview, makes identifying this family as my ancestors very unlikely.

Helpful Tip # 14 Do Not Click Links

If you do not have a paid subscription with Ancestry, do not click on the following links in your result matches: <u>View Record</u>, <u>View</u> <u>Image</u>, <u>Location</u>, <u>city</u>, <u>date</u>, <u>Year</u>, <u>race</u>, <u>relation</u>, <u>See all information...</u>, or <u>more</u>. These links will take you to a sign-up page that requires you to give them your credit card number for a "14 Day FREE trial". The downfall is that this subscription is difficult to cancel, ending up in monthly charges.

Although most researchers recommend that you begin with the 1930 census and work your way back in time, I have found no benefit for researching like this. For example, I have found only 1 unlikely record for "Holmer", 0 records for "DuBrill", "Kloko" and "Bowersox". And, too many records for "Reed" because it is too common. The Index for the 1930 Census did not benefit me very well.

However, when I repeated my search (by following the same instructions above, EXCEPT clicking on the link for the 1920 United States Federal Census in the "Included Data Collections" section instead), I found the following result matches: (5)

View Record	Arthur Holmer	Walter Helen	city Cook Illinois	abt 1918
View Record	Albert Holmer	Walter Helen	city Cook	abt 1920
			Illinois	

When I scrolled over the View Record link, I got the census preview:

```
Name:     Albert Holmer
Age:      0
Estimated abt 1920
birth year:
```

Comparing the preview to my age chart, the difference between the ages is 1 year, which is normal. This, combined with the fact that grandpa grew up in Chicago with Walter and Helen as his parents, makes identifying this family as my ancestors extremely likely. To be sure, I edited my search by adding "Cook County, Illinois, USA" to Location under Event Lived In and "albert arthur" to siblings, which gave me two additional result matches:

```
View    Helen Walter   city        abt
Record  Holmer         Cook        1899
                       Illinois

View    Walter name    city        abt
Record  Holmer name    Cook        1894
               Helen   Illinois
```

Comparing this preview to my age chart, the difference between the ages for Helen is two years, which is acceptable. I am convinced that I have identified this family as my ancestors. And, I added the new information to my age chart, as well as the location, so that it now looks like this:

```
Holmer,
  Walter    6     16     26     36
  Helen     3     13     23     33
  Arthur    -     --      2     12
  Albert    -     --      1     11
                         IL
```

I have identified three other families from the 1920 Census Index. I found Rlama Dubrill (abt 1910) with Myrtle A in Berrien County, Michigan. I also found Ervin

Kloko (abt 1900) with father, Herman E (abt 1862); mother, Minnie (abt 1861); and sibling, Edward (abt 1887) in St Joseph County, Michigan. Also, in St Joseph County, was Bernice Bowersox (abt 1902) with parents, Allen (abt 1873) and Orpha (abt 1880) and siblings: Ethel, Helen, Lucile, Ruth and Russell (abt 1901, 1905, 1908, 1911 and 1913, respectively).

Viewing Census Records

Although you will receive all the genealogical information that you need from free online indexes, there are a couple advantages to paying for a subscription to view the actual census. These advantages change depending on the census year. For example, you can see whether your ancestors had a radio set in 1930 or whether your ancestor's right to vote was denied on grounds other than criminal in 1870. By the following groupings, I have listed the biggest advantage for each census year to help you with this purchasing decision.

1900-1930 U.S. Federal Censuses

The biggest advantage of the 1900 census is the additional information of the person's date of birth by month and year. For example, I found out that my great-great grandfather, Herman Kloko, was born in April of 1860 and my great-great grandmother, Minnie, was born in October of 1861. I also found out that my great-great-great uncle, Chris Kloko, was born in February of 1855 and that my great-great-great aunt, Henrietta, was born in December of 1861.(6,7) These dates are important because they verify the accuracy of <u>birth</u> information.

The biggest advantage of the 1910 census is the additional information of whether a person was a survivor of the Union or Confederate Army or Navy, which means he should be recorded on the 1890 Veterans Schedule! This information is also important because it will help in future searches for military records.

The biggest advantage of the 1920 census is the additional information of the year of naturalization. For example, I found out that my great-great grandfather, John Holmer, was naturalized in 1886, two years after he immigrated to the United States from Sweden. I also found out that my great-great grandfather, Wojceich Szczesniak, was naturalized in 1893, three years after he immigrated to the United States from Poland.(8,9) Both these dates are important because they aid in researching immigration, emmigration and naturalization records.

The biggest advantage of the 1930 census is the additional information of age at first marriage. For example, I found out that my great grandmother, Myrtle, was 24 at her first marriage in 1909, which would be with my great grandfather, Allen DuBreuil. I also found out that my great grandmother, Josephine, was first married at the age of 20 in 1926, which would be with my great grandfather, William Reed. But, William was first married when he was 19 in 1917, which means he had a previous marriage that should be recorded for the 1920 census!(10,11) These three dates are also important because they verify the accuracy of marriage records.

Helpful Tip # 15 Find 1890 Veterans Schedules

The 1890 Veterans Schedule is a census of surviving

soldiers, sailors, marines and widows. Other information includes: rank, company, regiment or vessel, date of enlistment, date of discharge, Post Office address and whether a disability was incurred. These schedules are important because a fire destroyed almost the entire 1890 United States Federal Census.

1850-1880 U.S. Federal Censuses

The biggest advantage of the 1850 and 1860 censuses is the additional information from listing the names of every person in the family. For example, I found out that Clark Sandman, unrelated, was living in my great-great-great grandfather Wesley Cross' household. I also found out that the household, where my great-great-great-great grandmother Polly was living, was a relation, my great-great-great-great uncle Abner Cross.(12,13) This additional information is important because it enables easier family tracking through census records and narrows future searches of family records.

The biggest advantage of the 1870 census is the additional information of parentage for father and mother of foreign birth. For example, I found out from the parentage of my great-great-great grandfather Wesley Cross, that my great-great-great-great grandfather was not born of foreign birth. I also found out that my great-great-great-great grandmother was born in Canada with the parentage of both father and mother being of foreign birth.(14) This information is important because it narrows future searches for both foreign and domestic records.

The biggest advantage of the 1880 census is the additional information of street names and house numbers for each family. This additional information is important because it enables us to find the exact building that our relatives inhabited, if it is still standing.

Helpful Tip # 16 FREE 1870 Michigan Census

The Library of Michigan made the 1870 U.S. Federal Census of Michigan free and available for research. Although the Library of Michigan has been the victim of state budget cuts, online digital images of the census can still be found in other searchable databases. Copies of transcriptions of the census can also be found in the reference section of any Michigan library.

1790-1840 U.S. Federal Censuses

Although census records have their many advantages, one disadvantage of the 1790-1840 censuses is that they only list the head of the family instead of the individual household members. Also, changes in each census, going back in time, seems to get more difficult for family identification. There is little distinction between relations, residing visitors and domestic help who are free white persons. There is even less distinction between slaves and freed colored persons.

Remember

Don't forget to update your age chart, filling in locations from the online indexes and any new names that you might have come across. After omitting the individual names and ages to save space here in this book, my chart looked something like this:

DAVID HOLMER

	1850	1860	1870	1880	
Holmer,	X	X	X	X	
Szczesniak,		X	X	X	IL
DuBreuil,	NY	IL	IN	IL	
Cross,		MI	MI	MI	MI
Reed,		?	IN	IN	IN
Leggett,	?	?	?	?	
Kloko,		X	NY	MI	MI
Bowersox	PA	PA	MI	MI	

	1900	1910	1920	1930	
Holmer,	IL	IL	IL	IL	
Szczesniak,		IL	IL	IL	IL
DuBreuil,	IL	IL	?	?	
Cross,		MI	IL	?	MI
Reed,		IN	IN	MI	MI
Leggett,	?	MI	MI	MI	
Kloko,		MI	MI	MI	IN
Bowersox	MI	MI	MI	MI	

Chapter 5
"Vital Records"

County Clerks

With conflicts between our right to privacy and our constitutional right to inspect government documents, genealogists rely on the county clerk's administrative rules for access to vital records. These records can be divided into two categories: death & marriage records (which courts consider the public's limited right to inspect outweighs the right to privacy) and birth records (which courts consider the right to privacy outweighs the public's limited right to inspect). Although there are some limits, each county clerk ultimately defines these limitations.

For example: Michigan's Berrien County is very pro-family with their genealogical access to records. "All marriage and death indexes are open for all records regardless of age, and all records that are more than 75 years of age are open for public inspection. Also, for records that are less than 75 years of age, an application can be filled out for inspection of a specific record."(15) Michigan's Van Buren County is not as generous, only allowing open access to the marriage and death indexes. "Inspection of death and marriage records or libers are only permitted after paying a $1.00 search fee AND the record can not be located in the space specified by the Index."(16) Michigan's Grand Traverse County Clerk is anti-family and genealogy with a strict NO access to records or Indexes. However, they do "allow you to purchase certified copies of records, if you already know the person you're looking for."(17)

Helpful Tip # 17 Call Ahead of Time

Some county clerks have specific days and times for genealogical research. Some county clerks have seperate buildings for older, archived records or seperate departments for marriage records. Some states hold vital records at a health department instead of the county clerk. And, finding current county clerk information online is rare. Calling ahead of time can also answer quick questions as to what you need to bring, ie. identification and proper payment!

County Clerks also have other administrative rules that can affect your genealogical research. Although open access may be granted for inspecting indexes and records, some county clerks require identification to obtain a copy of records. Payment for these copies also varies between clerk offices. Copy prices vary between $1.00 to $20.00, depending on whether a genealogical or non-certified record is available. (Currently, Michigan law does not allow non-certified copies) And, form of payment can even vary between different departments.

For example, Illinois' Cook County Clerk's office does NOT take checks, Visa or Visa Debit cards; only cash, MasterCard, MasterCard Debit, and American Express are accepted. However, checks are accepted by Illinois' Cook County Clerk when ordering a copy of a record by mail.

Helpful Tip # 18 Get Death Records

You need a death record to obtain access to birth and some marriage records. For most counties, you can look up the record from indexes or libers. For counties that restrict access or require exact dates, you can get a close enough date usually from cemetery records that record the burial date to obtain a death record.

There are many benefits to obtaining death records. Foremost is that it identifies you as an "heir". In accordance with federal and state laws, any heir with a certified death certificate is granted certified copies of the birth record. Most county clerks interpret the law as also granting copies of any marriage or divorce records.

Using Indexes and Libers

Indexes and Libers are those large, old books first used to record births, deaths, marriages, property ownership, and tax rolls. They can usually be identified by their huge size of 15x24 and 4" thick. The sheer weight of these books requires a special shelving unit that holds them horizontal and usually has rollers to aid in their retreiving. The indexes are recorded alphebetically and libers are recorded chronologically. It is usually best to start with the index.

For example, I started with the death indexes. I began with our surname, Bauman. I found 13 deaths under that surname in the first index. Then, I looked up possible alternate spellings from my list of surnames. I found one death under Baumen and another under Bouman.(18) Using my notebook and a pencil, I recorded my findings in a short list:

```
Bauman, August F       3 - 29
Bauman, Chas. A        2 - 219
Bauman, Fred           1 - 158
Bauman, Frederika      2 - 12
Bauman, Geo.           2 - 51
Bauman, Indiana Hilinda
                       3 - 201
Bauman, Jacob          2 - 49
Bauman, John           3 - 219
Bauman, Lena           3 - 132
Bauman, Sophia         1 - 99
Bauman, Sophia         2 - 126
Bauman, Sophia         2 - 29
Bauman, Susanah        1 - 99
Baumen, Fred           2 - 67
Bouman, Geo W          3 - 11
```

The index lists the name followed by the liber number, the number of the book containing the record, and the page number. I had traced my Bauman ancestry back to a Fred and Sophia, but the index listed two Freds and three Sophias. Luckily, the Saint Joseph County Clerk grants access to Death Libers, saving me costly research if I had to purchase a certified copy of each record. The following records were in the first death liber:(19)

```
16   Feb 16 1877   Bauman Sophia F - married
     68 Fawn River MI   cancer   Germany

13   Sep 18 1882   Bauman Frederick M W married
     66-5-6 Sherman MI apoplexy Germany
```

The liber lists a line number followed by the date of death, name of the deceased, sex, race or color, marital status, age, location of death, cause of death, and birthplace. The age can be listed as a single number, such as 68, or as a combination number, such as 66-5-6, representing the age in years, months and days. From this combination number a date of birth can be calculated, such as Apr 12 1816 for the case of Frederick Bauman (above).

Comparing the first death record to my age chart, the difference between the ages of both Sophias is 11 years. Usually, the age differs by only about 2-3 years. This, combined with the fact that the census location and location of death are not a match and that the date of death preceeds the 1880 census, makes identifying this person as my ancestor very unlikely.

On the other hand, the second death record, which is within 1 year of my age chart and the location of death matches the 1880 US Census, is extremely likely to be my ancestor. The marital status records Fred Bauman as married, suggesting that Sophia was still alive at his time of death. The following records were in the second death liber:(20)

```
173  Dec 17 1895 Bauman Sophia F W widowed
     75-6-25 Sherman - Germany

4    Dec 27 1898 Bauman Fred M W married
     49-5-5 Sherman apoplexy Germany

94   Apr 25 1903 Bauman Sophia F W widowed
     49-8-16 Sherman apoplexy Germany
```

Comparing these records to my age charts confirms that these are my ancestors from Sherman, MI: Sophia, the mother and wife of Fred from the earlier record in book one; Fred, the son of Sophia; and, Sophia, Fred's wife, respectively.

Certified Copy of Records of Deaths

These certificates are obtained from the County Clerk when the record of death is contained in a liber. They can usually be recognized as a typed standard form and a certification of the form with date, signature and seal of the deputy clerk. The information on these forms include name of deceased, date and place of death, cause of death, and age. They may also include occupation, birthplace, and parents if known.

The accuracy of birth dates, birthplaces, and parents are usually unreliable if the death occurred at an older age. For example, if the deceased was a child, the reliability of the parental and birth information is much more accurate than if the deceased was 100 years old. The accuracy of translation is also unreliable as it is passed from physician to county clerk to liber to form. Mistakes and misspellings can often happen, but the death information can be accepted as most accurate.

Certificate and Records of Deaths

These certificates are obtained from the County Clerk when the death certificate has been recorded by means of microfilm or microfiche. They can usually be recognized as a photocopy of a record and a certification of the copy with date, signature and seal of the deputy clerk. The information on these forms include the name of the deceased, date and place of death, diagnosis and physician information, burial and mortician information. They may also contain occupation, birth and parental information if known.

The disadvantage of these certificates is that they can sometimes be difficult to read from poor photocopying. Clerks try to do their best at getting the most readable copy available for you. The advantage is that this is a copy of the actual form filled out by the physician and there is much less inaccuracies due to translation.

Helpful Tip # 19 Copy Your Originals

Because Certified Records and Certified Copies of Records ARE legal documents, you need to protect them from damage or loss. For the best protection, COPY the original record for your genealogy. On the copy in permanent RED ink write "Copy". Only keep those copies with your genealogy. Originals should always be locked away in a safe place!

Marriage Licenses

These certificates are sent to the couple from the Clerk of the County where the marriage occurred upon certification. They can usually be recognized from the ornamental calligraphy and a horizontal division seperating the license portion of the certificate from the certification portion. The information on these licenses include: bride's name, age, residence; groom's name, age, residence; date of license and deputy clerk; date of marriage, place of marriage, officiate and church.

Licenses are usually accurate records for marriages. They are usually hand written by both a deputy clerk (for the licensing part) and an officiate (for the ceremonial part). However, mistakes occasionally do happen, which may include: unreadable information, misspelled name or part of a name, use of a nickname and/or use of an uncommon abbreviation. Despite the difficulty of reading, these documents are legal and contain all pertinent information about the marriage for genealogical purposes.

Duplicate License and Certificate of Marriages

These certificates are sent to the couple from the person solemnizing the marriage upon receipt of original from the Clerk of the County where the marriage occurred. They can usually be recognized from the golden County seal and a horizontal division seperating the license portion of the certificate from the certification portion. The information on these certificates includes more specifics, like color or race, occupations, father names, mother maiden names, number of previous marriages and/or addresses of the witnesses.

Duplicates are the most accurate record of a marriage. They are filled out by all three parties (bride, groom and officiate), approved by the deputy clerk within 30 days of marriage and recorded shortly thereafter. Mistakes rarely happen because of the approval requirements to obtain the license and that the license itself expires, becoming void after 30 days of being issued. Despite of being ideal for genealogical purposes, these duplicates are the legal document for the marriage, making them very hard to come by.

Helpful Tip # 20 Get Marriage Applications

Some county clerks make a distinction between the actual marriage record and the marriage application. The application for marriage is the portion that is a seperation of bride and groom information. This contains birth, parental and occupational information, as well as, any information about previous marriages.

Certified Copy of Record of Marriages

These certificates are obtained from the Clerk of the County where the marriage is recorded in a liber. They can usually be recognized as a typed form and a certification of the form with date, signature and seal of a deputy clerk. The information on these certificates includes: full name, age, race, residence, birthplace, occupation, name of father, maiden name of mother, number of previous marriages for both the groom and the bride; date of license, date of marriage, place of marriage, officiate, witnesses, witnessess residences and/or date of record.

The accuracy of certified copies of records are unreliable. They are usually forms filled out by a deputy clerk by deciphering a handwritten County Liber, which was copied from marriage licenses decades earlier. Mistakes often happen, which may include: unreadable information, misspellings, incorrect dates and/or ommission of unknown information. Despite the frequency of mistakes, these documents are a legal attempt to record all possible information about a marriage, and can be obtained for a fee from any branch for that county clerk.

Certified Copy of Record of Births

These certificates are obtained from the Clerk of the County where the birth is recorded in a liber. They can usually be recognized as a typed form and a certification of the form with date, signature and seal of a deputy clerk. The information on these certificates include: name at birth, sex, place of birth, mother's maiden name, mother's birthplace, father's name, father's birthplace and date of record.

The accuracy of certified copies of records are unreliable. They are usually forms filled out by a deputy clerk by deciphering a handwritten County Liber, which was copied from Health Department Registers decades earlier. Mistakes often happen, which may include: unreadable information, misspellings, incorrect dates and/or ommission of unknown information. Despite of the frequency of mistakes, these documents are legal, attempt to record all possible information about a birth, and can be obtained for a fee from any branch for that county clerk.

Certificate of Births and Certificate of Live Births

These certificates are obtained from the Clerk of the County where the birth certificate is recorded on microfilm or microfiche. They can usually be recognized as a copy of an original record and a certification of the document with date, signature and seal of a deputy clerk. The information on these certificates includes more specifics, like number of births, order of births, parent's occupation and parent's places of birth.

Certificate of births are usually accurate records for name, date of birth and parental information. They are usually copied from microfiche, microfilm, digital or original records, which was submitted to the county. However, mistakes occasionally do happen, which may include: a mispelled name, part of a name and/or parent name. Despite of the difficulty of copying and reading, these documents are legal and contain the most accurate of records obtainable from a county clerk.

Helpful Tip # 21 Cut Off Certifications

Certified copies of records and certificates ARE legal and contain a certification by the county clerk. Certified birth records are even more important as they are proof of identification and can be used fraudulently. When copying and marking copies with RED ink (from Helpful Tip #19 above), cut off the certification part of the genealogy copy as an added precaution!

Remember

Don't forget to update your ancestor chart, filling in dates and any new names that you might have come across from all of your research. After researching, my chart now looks something like this:

```
     (Fourth Generation)
  8  Austin W Holmer (1893-1967)
  9  Helen I Szczesniak (1897-1968)
 10  Allan L DuBreuil (1883-1917)
 11  Myrtle A Cross (1884-1951)
 12  William Reed (1897-1976)
 13  Josephine E Leggett (1906-1998)
 14  Ervin L Kloko (1899-1949)
 15  Bernice O Bowersox (1902-1957)
```

(Fifth Generation)
16 John Holmer (1866-?)
17 Emilia Holmer (1870-?)
18 Wojceich Szczesniak (1873-1947)
19 Malgorzata Szczesniak (1869-1930)
20 William A DuBreuil (1809-1899)
21 Martha J DuBreuil (1852-1920)
22 Eugene Cross (1854-?)
23 Charlotte Briggs (1860-?)
24 Ezra Reed (1850-?)
28 Herman Kloko (1860-?)
29 Minnie Kloko (1861-?)
30 Allen Bowersox (1872-1943)
31 Orpha J Bowersox (1878-1929)

(Sixth Generation)
40 Augustus DuBreuil (1821-1875)
41 Elizabeth DuBreuil (1832-?)
44 Wesley Cross (1819-?)
45 Caroline Cross (1822-1915)
46 James Briggs (1830-?)
47 Eliza Briggs (1840-?)
56 Frederick Kloko (1832-?)
57 Mary Kloko (1818-?)
60 S. J. Bowersox (1845-?)
61 Lydia Bowersox (1844-?)

Chapter 6
"Read All About It"

Newspapers

One of the more difficult resources to locate and utilize is newspaper articles. These difficulties can range from newspapers going out of business or downsizing to articles being found on fragile papers, microfilm or microfiche. Another difficulty is the search for an article can be tedious if you do not already know the exact date of the event you are looking for. However, newspapers can be much more personable, as well as helpful.

To begin looking for newspaper articles, use your favorite search engine and type in the word *newspapers* along with the county name and state from locations of your US Census findings. Be sure to review all results of your search to compose a more complete listing of all newspapers within a certain location. For example, the search of "Berrien County Michigan newspapers" resulted the following list:

```
Benton Spirit
Berrien County Record
Harbor Country News
Herald-Palladium
Niles Daily Star
Student Movement
Tri-City Record
```

This list will most likely consist of current newspapers, which would be able to be contacted in order to gain further information. When contacting these newspapers be sure to be clear on what you are looking for. For example, the Herald-

Palladium offers an online archive of their newspaper; however, this archive consists only of papers within the past two weeks/14 days.(21) If the newspaper does not offer an on-site or online archive, they can usually direct you to where one is.

Helpful Tip # 22 Visit Local Libraries

Many newspapers send their archived papers to the local library because these archives are in the form of microfilm or microfiche. Libraries are an excellent place to view these archives, since they usually already have the viewer/ projector. Local libraries also tend to store older newspapers that are no longer in circulation, especially if they have a local history/genealogy room for these fragile papers.

Microfiche

Microfiche can be recognized as thin, square plastic films that can be placed on a glass tray to be read. Microfiche viewers are typically easy to use by scrolling right, left, up or down. Focusing the viewer is similar to focusing a microscope by moving the lens closer and farther away from the glass plate. Although some viewers are easier to read in the negative, making a photocopy of any articles will be easier to read if they are in the typical black print with white background.

Microfilm

Microfilm can be recognized as a roll of film on a small reel that can be fed through a projector to be read. Microfilm viewers/projectors are typically a little harder to get use to because you scroll side to side and roll to go up and down.

Also, depending on the dates of the reel and the date you are looking for, it may still take some time to reel through the roll to find the location of the newspaper. Again, making a photocopy would read easier if made in black print with a white background.

Births

Birth lisitngs usually include: the name of the hospital, the full name of the newborn, the sex of the newborn, the names of the proud parents, their residence, the date and time of birth, and the weight of the newborn at birth. Some listings may also include the names and residences of the proud grandparents.

Helpful Tip # 23 Check Hospital Section

Some newspapers have a seperate section for hospital listings. This is the section where you will most likely find birth listings. Other listings here include: admissions and discharges. Sometimes, newspapers only print this section accumatively, usually once a week.

Engagements, Marriages & Divorces

Engagement and marriage listings usually include: names and location of both individuals, names and location of their parents, date and place of marriage, names and locations of witnesses and pastor officiating the ceremony. Older listings have also included: graduation information, employment information, and wedding specifics (flowers, decorations, bridal description, etc.). For example, the newspaper article on my grandparents' wedding reads:

```
Doris Kloko and William Reed
   Are Wed in Home Rites
```

Miss Doris Kloko, daughter of Mr. and Mrs. Irvin Kloko, 928 South Lincoln avenue, and William Reed, son of Mr. and Mrs. William Reed, Sr., rural route three, were united in marriage at 7 p.m. Saturday.

The Rev. Anthony J. Martin, pastor of Coulter's chapel, performed the ceremony beneath an arch of red roses and white satin bows set in the Kloko home for the ceremony. Giant chrysanthemums and baby mums completed the decorations.

The bride wore a blue and white suit with brown accessories and a corsage of gardenias and Talisman roses for the ceremony, and her attendant, Mrs. Kenneth Kloko, wore a brown gabardine suit with yellow and brown accessories and a corsage of red roses. Kenneth Kloko, brother of the bride, was best man.

About 35 guests were received at a reception following the ceremony in the Kloko home and a tiered wedding cake centered the bride's table. Both are graduates of Niles high school and the groom is a navy veteran. (22)

Divorce listings usually include: county of divorce, full names of both individuals, custody of children and maiden name (if restored by court). Older divorce filings have also included: city location of both individuals, charges for divorce, and marriage date and location. For example, the newspaper article on my grandparents' divorce reads:

```
FILES FOR DIVORCE
```

Doris Reed, Niles, filed for divorce in Berrien county circuit court Wednesday afternoon against William Reed, Jr., of Niles. She charged cruelty and non-support, ans asked custody of a daughter. They were married Oct., 23, 1948, in Niles, and seperated last Thursday. (23)

Helpful Tip # 24 Check the Court Section
Some newspapers have a section for court listings. These

listings of genealogical interest include: divorce filings, marriage license applications, real estate transfers and estate settlements. Other listings may include: civil law suit settlements, police reports, traffic ticketing and fines, and criminal charges.

Death Notices and Obituaries

Death notices are short listings, usually published free of charge and include: name of deceased, age, city location, date of death, name and relationship of surviving family members and information on both visitation and services. For example, the newspaper notice about my great aunt reads:

```
Infant Rites

Prayer Services were held this afternoon at 3 at Silverbrook
cemetery for Mary Kloko who was still born to Mr. and Mrs.
Ervin Kloko, 928 South Lincoln avenue, this morning at 3.

The infant is survived by her parents, four brothers,
Kenneth, Dale, Wesley, and Paul, and two sisters, Beulah and
Doris. The Rev. Floyd Johnston officiated at services.(24)
```

Obituaries are longer listings, which are special tributes purchased by family and friends, and usually include: name of deceased, residence, length of residency, birth information, parent names, marriage information, occupations, religious and community affiliations, hobbies, name and relationship of surviving family members, name and relationship of family members preceding the death and information on both visitation and services. Older obituaries have also included immigration information and family stories. For example, the newspaper obituary for my great-great grandmother reads:

Mrs. Wilhelmina Kloko

CENTERVILLE, Mich., Feb. 11.-- (Special) --
Mrs. Wilhelmina Fredericka Carolene Kloko, 74, died here
Sunday at the home of her daughter, Mrs. Ella Hazel.

Mrs, Kloko was born October 24, 1861, in Pomerania, Germany,
a daughter of Frederick and Sophia Bauman, and came to
America with her parents in 1864. The trip in a sailboat took
six weeks. The family came to St. Joseph county and settled
on a farm at Fish Lake, Sherman township.

Mrs. Kloko was married August 25, 1883, to Herman Kloko, who
died September 18, 1921. For the last 12 years she had made
her home with her daughter, Mrs. Ella Hazel. She is survived
by three daughters, Mrs. Henry Kramer, Sturgis; Mrs, Ella
Hazel, Centerville, and Mrs. Vern Depue, Mendon, and one son,
Ervin Kloko, Niles. (25)

Helpful Tip # 25 Check the Headlines

Many newspapers fill their headlines with breaking
local news. These local headlines are usually "good news"
events like: golden anniversaries, family business success
stories, and the happy return of a loved one. Sometimes,
these headlines are catastrophic like the first traffic fatality in
three years. Each of these articles may hold a large variety of
genealogical information from new names to dates.

Chapter 7
"Other Records"

Alternate Sources

There are many other records that are just as beneficial to genealogical research as vital records. Sometimes, these records are more personable and even more accurate than the ones from the county clerk's office. The disadvantages of these alternate sources are their inconsistencies in how they were maintained, assuming that they even existed in the first place. In addition, these sources can also be very difficult to find; however, they are usually with the family's keepsakes.

Death Documents

Alternate death documents can vary depending on a family's tradition and religious affiliation. Ceremonies customary to these traditions usually dictate as to whether documents exist--and, if so, which ones. Finding these other documents also depends on your family's tradition; however, copies are most likely found wherever that person's last effects are.

Funeral Memory Folders

These cards are handed out to friends and family at the time of the memorial service. They can be recognized as a folder/card with a simple picture on the front with words like In Remembrance, In Memoriam, or In Loving Memory. The information inside these cards include: the name of the deceased; the date of birth; the date of death; information about the place, date and time of service; the name of the officiating clergyman; and the place of internment. These cards may also include: the place of birth, the place of death and pallbearers.

Memory folders are the most personable record of death. They usually include a biblical passage, poem, prayer and/ or saying that encompasses what the family and their loved one believed. However, funeral memorials have some disadvantages, which may include: omission of internment or burial information, error or misprint in date of birth and/or date of death, and/or unreadable printing.

Memorial Prayer Cards

These cards are handed out to family and friends at the time of the memorial mass or service. They can be recognized as 2x4 inch cards with a pictorial of the blessed Mary, Jesus or one of the saints on the front. The information on the reverse of these cards include: name of the deceased, date of birth, date of death and a prayer. They may also include: service information, internment information and funeral home information.

Prayer cards are the most religious record of death. The picture has special meaning like The Good Shepherd, Jesus carrying a lamb through the fold's threshhold, symbolizes Christ's divinity. Some pictures represent a special devotion like the Immaculate Heart of Mary, a flaming heart surrounded by roses, which symbolizes love and devotion to Jesus and God. These cards have some disadvantages, which may include: error, misprint, or omission of some information and/or printed in the language of the church (ie., Latin) or language of the family.

Helpful Hint # 25 Look in Prayer Books/ Missals

"If you ever find an old Catholic missal, you will likely find several prayer cards stuffed inside."(26) These books may also contain pictures of relatives needing special prayer, like an illness, or signs of something the family was struggling with, like a bill that demonstrates financial hardships needing special prayer. A church bulletin kept between the pages may have a special meaning for the family during a specific time period. All these items can be helpful in your genealogy and make it more personable at the same time.

Physician's Certificate of Deaths

These records are issued by the State Board of Health. They can be recognized as a short form, usually hand written, dated and signed by a physician. The information on this forms include: name of deceased, sex, color or race, age, occupation, date of death, marrital status, nationality, length of residence, place of death, cause of death, duration of disease, place of burial and name of undertaker.

Physician's certificate is the most accurate record of death. They are filled out at the time of death by the attending physician. However, these certificates have some disadvantages, which may include: unreadable handwriting, discrepency in the age, omission of nationality and/or length of residence.

Marriage Documents

Alternate marriage documents can vary depending on a family's tradition. Ceremonies customary to these traditions usually dictate as to whether documents exist--and, if so, which ones. Finding these other documents also depends upon your family's tradition; however, they are most likely to be found with the family's albums or scrapbooks.

Marriage Invitation Announcements

These invites are handed out to friends and family from the parents of the bride sometime before the wedding. They can usually be recognized as a folder/card with a short announcement. The information on these cards include: parent names, name of the bride, name of the groom, date (time) of the marriage, place of marriage, church and/or parent/reception address.

The accuracy of invitation announcements are unreliable. They are usually printed in advance, well before the actual marriage takes place. Mistakes often happen, which may include: misprints, use of name from previous marriage, marriage did not take place, incorrect date due to delay or weather and/or incorrect place due to delay or weather. Despite of not being a legal proof or reliable source of a marriage, these cards are good to use as a possible lead in searching for better verification.

Marriage Certificates or Bridal Tokens

These certificates are handed out to the bride from the officiate at the time of marriage. They can usually be recognized from the flower design and ornamental calligraphy prominently displayed on the front with a fancy protective cover on the back. The information on these certificates vary depending on the stock and may contain: groom's name, groom's residence, bride's name, bride's residence, date of marriage, place of marriage, witnesses signatures, officiate's signature and/or church.

Certificates or bridal tokens are usually accurate records for marriages. They are usually hand written by the officiate and signed by the witnesses afterwards. However, mistakes could happen, like the use of a name from a previous marriage or unreadable information. Despite of these possible mistakes and not being legal proof of a marriage, these certificates are ideal for genealogical purposes with the added personal benefit of having signature of those who actually witnessed the marriage!

Helpful Tip # 26 Look in Wedding Keepsakes

You can usually find the Bridal Token or Marriage Certificate in the person's wedding keepsake along with one of the marriage announcement folders that the parents sent out. These will provide you will the most accurate marriage information. You may also find an actual family tree or genealogical record filled out for both the groom's family and the bride's family, additionally giving you the names of parents, grandparents and great-grandparents.

Birth Documents

Alternate birth documents can vary depending on a family's history and tradition. The type of birth usually dictates what type of documents exist. Finding this type of documentation depends on how well it was maintained; and, copies are most likely found wherever that person's last effects are. Tradition can also affect what types of documents there are. These documents are most likely found with the family albums.

Birth Announcements

These cards are handed out to friends and family from the parents around the time of birth. They can usually be recognized as a folder/card with a photograph inside. The information on these cards include: the baby's name, date of birth, weight and parent names.

Birth announcements are the most accurate record of birth names. They are usually written by the person who actually gave the name (ie. mother or father). However, birth announcements have some disadvantages, which may include: unreadable handwriting, omission of surname, omission of one or both parent names and/or discrepency in the date of birth. Despite of not being a legal proof of birth, these cards are ideal for genealogical purposes with the added personal benefit of having the baby's first picture included!

Birth Records and Hospital Birth Certificates

These certificates are handed out at the hospital at the time of birth. They can usually be recognized from the hospital's name, address and gold seal prominantly displayed on the front with ink prints on the back. The information on these certificates vary depending on the hospital and may contain: birth name, parent names, time and date of birth, county, color or race, sex, weight and signature of physician, superindendent and/or hospital administrator.

Birth records are the most accurate record of time and date of birth. They are usually filled out and signed by an actual attendant of the birth (ie. physician or nurse). However, birth records have some disadvantages, which may include: omission of one or both parent names and/ or discrepency in the name given at birth. Despite of not being a legal proof of birth, these certificates are ideal for genealogical purposes with the added personal benefit of having the baby's first footprints included!

Helpful Tip # 27 Look in Baby Books

You can usually find the Birth Record or Hospital Birth Certificate in the person's baby book along with one of the baby announcements that the parents sent out. Together, these will provide you with the most accurate name and date (time) of birth. You may also find an actual Family tree or genealogical record filled out, additionally giving you the names of parents, grandparents, and great-grandparents!

Notification of Birth Registrations

These certificates are sent to the mother from the Department of Health upon registration of birth. They can usually be recognized from the State's seal and Health Commissioner's signature prominently displayed on the front. The information on these certificates include: birth name, place of birth, date of birth, name of father and maiden name of mother.

Birth registrations are usually accurate records for name and date of birth. They are usually copied from parent and doctor by nurse to an official record, which is submitted and copied by a registrar. However, mistakes occasionally do happen, which may include: a misspelled name, part of a name and/or parent name. Despite of the lack of additional details and any personal benefits, these documents are legal and contain all pertinent information for genealogical purposes.

Delayed Record of Births

These certificates are sent to the applicant from the Clerk of the County where the birth occurred upon research and approval. They can usually be recognized as a typed form and an affidavit on the document with date, signature and seal of a Notary Public. The information on these certificates can include: place of birth, name at birth, date of birth, color or race, sex, name changes, father's name and birthplace, mother's name and birthplace, and informant's name and address.

The accuracy of delayed records are unreliable. They are usually forms filled out after the attending physician and/ or parents have deceased by acquaintainces who verify someone's identity by swearing an oath. Mistakes often happen, which may include: incorrect birth name, incorrect date of birth and/or incorrect parent information. Despite of the frequency of mistakes, these documents are legal and attempt to record all possible information about a birth.

Helpful Tip # 28 Protect Your Legal Documents

Because birth registrations and delayed records ARE legal, you need to protect them against Identity Fraud. For the best protection, COPY the original record for your genealogy. On the copy in permanent RED ink write "Deceased" (for birth records of those who have already passed) or "For Genealogical Purposes Only" (for those who are still living). Only keep those copies with your genealogy. Originals should always be locked away in a safe place!

Remember

Don't forget to update your ancestor chart, filling in dates and any new names that you might have come across from all of your research. After researching, my chart now looks something like this:

```
    (Fifth Generation)
16  John E Holmer (1863-1933)
17  Anna E Anderson (1870-1944)
18  Adalbert Szczesniak (1873-1947)
19  Malgorzata Dominiak (1869-1930)
20  William A DuBreuil (1849-1916)
21  Martha J Holbrook (1852-1920)
22  Eugene Cross (1854-?)
23  Charlotte Briggs (1860-?)
24  Ezra Reed (1860-1936)
25  Sarah Harter (1866-1927)
26  Fred Leggett (1871-1951)
27  Bertha M Reinke (1874-1947)
28  Herman Kloko (1860-1921)
29  Wilhelmina F Bauman (1861-1936)
30  Allen Bowersox (1872-1943)
31  Orpha J Boudeman (1878-1929)

    (Sixth Generation)
32  Peter Holmer
33  Eleanor Youson
34  Nels Anderson
38  Pawel Dominiak
39  Malgorzata Dominiak
40  Augustus DuBreuil (1821-1875)
41  Elizabeth DuBreuil (1832-1892)
42  Joseph Holbrook (1814-1881)
43  Mary Holbrook (1817-1884)
44  Wesley Cross (1809-1899)
45  Caroline Pauling (1810-1915)
46  James Briggs (1832-1911)
47  Eliza Barber (1840-?)
48  Abel Reed (1821-?)
49  Millie A Reed (1832-?)
50  Manford Harter (1846-?)
51  Armilda Abbott (1848-?)
52  Jesse G Leggett (1836-1892)
53  Esther L Barnes (1834-1910)
54  Julius Reinke (1848-1934)
55  Augusta Able (1849-1937)
```

56 Frederick Kloko (1833-1899)
57 Mary Kuss (1818-1883)
58 Frederick Bauman (1816-1882)
59 Sophia Stry (1820-1895)
60 Solomon Bowersox (1845-1918)
61 Lydia Kerr (1843-1880)
62 Albert Boudeman (1846-1900)
63 Amanda Seas (1852-1921)

Chapter 8
"Research Standards"

Standard Forms

The easiest way to share your family genealogy with others is through the use of standardized forms. Although difficulties arise from trying to use these forms for adoptions or children out of wedlock, the advantage of finding what you need when you need it makes using the forms definitely worth it. For a large selection and variety of forms for genealogists to choose from, I recommend forms that I have found at cs.williams.edu/~bailey/genealogy/

Research Logs

These forms are used to record how genealogists do their research. They can usually be recognized as a lined paper with columns and a heading. The information on these forms include: name of person being researched, the source of information found (title/author, type, date), and comments or results of the research. They may also contain: objectives, dates of search, location or call numbers and documentation numbers.

The Works Cited appendix is a primitive form of the research log. It has helped us record the beginnings of our research. However, there are many benefits to using the standardized research logs for our continuing research. Foremost is that they are formatted to help focus on specific areas that need more research. As our collection of birth, death and marriage documents increase, research logs also enable us to quickly identify which vital records are still missing from our collection.

Helpful Tip # 29 Purchase a Firebox

Some documentation is more valuable than others, especially if it is an original document. Even if a document is a copy of an original, the cost of replacing it may make it just as valuable as an original. These valuable documents need to be preserved against damage from fire and water. The best investment for this type of protection is a good fire box.

Pedigree Charts

These forms are used to record a descendant's lineage. They can usually be recognized by the lines connecting ancestors together forming the *family tree*. The information on these forms include: names of ancestors, dates of births, dates of marriages, and dates of deaths. They may also contain: birthplaces, location of marriages, places of death and pictures of relatives.

The Ancestor Chart is a primitive form of the pedigree chart. It has helped us record the beginnings of our genealogy. However, there are many benefits to using the standardized pedigree charts for our continuing research. Foremost is that they are formatted with enough space to include additional information for births, deaths and marriages. Pedigree charts also enable us to quickly identify large gaps in our genealogical research.

Family Group Records

These forms are used to record information about a particular family. They can usually be recognized by its three sections for the Husband, the Wife, and the Children. The information on these forms include: birth dates and places, marriage dates and places, and death dates and places. The information in the husband and wife sections also contain: father's name, mother's name, and other wives or husbands. The information in the children sections also contain: name of spouse, birth and death of spouse, and name of spouse's parents.

The Age Chart is a primitive form of the family group record. It has helped us record the beginnings of our families by census locations. However, age charts are inadequate for continuing research. Although using family group records will greatly increase paperwork, they are extremely useful for the quick retrieval of genealogical information. The disadvantage of paperwork accumulation can be resolved with good storage organization.

Helpful Tip # 30 Use File Boxes

File boxes are useful for organizing the storage of all the Family Group records. When considering the type of file box needed, the short box works better than the deep because of the sheer weight after it is filled. The cardboard file box is also a good alternative because it is cheap enough to purchase right away and can be easily expanded upon as your research continues to grow.

Writing Names

The standard for recording a person's name is the full first name followed by the full middle name(s) followed by the full last name or surname in capital letters. Other standards apply when there are more than one name for an individual. Generally, females are recorded with their maiden name

(name before marriage) used. Adoptions and name changes have been left to the discretion of the genealogist. For example:

>Albert Walter HOLMER
>Rhama Alene DuBREUIL
>William REED Jr
>Doris Arleen KLOKO

When multiple generations use the same name, the standard for recording the name is as follows: the first generation omits the suffix, Sr (senior) or I; the following generations retain the suffix as Jr (junior) or the corresponding Roman numeral. An example of this is Albert Holmer Sr and William Reed Jr, above. There are also other abbreviations associated with people that are used in genealogy. For Example:

>d/o - daughter of
>s/o - son of
>w/o - wife of

Helpful Tip # 31 Recycle Recipe Boxes

Old recipe boxes can be recycled into great reference tools with the use of index cards. Arranging the index cards by surnames can aid in the quick retrieval of family or census information. Arranging the cards by location can aid in quick referencing for cemetery or record research. Recycled boxes are also useful as a roll-a-dex of living family members for reunions and get-togethers.

Recording Dates

The standard for recording a date in genealogy is the day with one or two digits followed by the month either spelled out fully or using a three letter abbreviation followed by the full year using four digits. Other standards apply when the exact date is not known. Generally, a hyphen is used when a time period can be determined. For example:

> March 1919
> 01 JAN 1910
> abt 1920s
> bet 1929-1932

When approximations are used for dates, the standard for recording these dates are to use the following abbreviations: abt, for events about this date; aft, for events after this date; bef, for events before this date; and bet, for events between these dates. There are also other abbreviations associated with dates that are used in genealogy. For example:

> b - date of birth
> d - date of death
> m - date of marriage
> m2- date of second marriage
> B - date of baptism
> bur- date of burial or internment
> div- date of divorce

Standards for Places

The standard for recording a place in genealogy is the full name of the township or city followed by the full name of the county followed by the name of abbreviation for the state or providence followed by the name or abbreviation for the country. Generally, full names are used when the providence or country is less familiar. For example:

> South Chicago, Cook, IL, USA
> Chicago, Cook, IL, USA
> Niles, Berrien, Michigan, USA
> Valparaiso, Porter, Indiana, USA

When other countries are used, the standard for recording these places are to use the following abbreviations: SWE, for Sweden; POL, for Poland; CAN, for Canada; WAL, for Wales; ENG, for England; IRE, for Ireland; GER, for Germany; FRA, for France; and DEN, for Denmark. There are also other abbreviations associated with places that are used in genealogy. For example:

> p - place
> bp- place of birth
> dp- place of death
> cem- cemetery location

Helpful Tip # 32 Reserve Adequate Storage

Genealogy can be viewed as the ultimate collection with vast amount of information in the form of keepsakes and documentation. The largest amount of storage should be reserved for keepsakes, which are often bulky. To help reduce this bulk, it may be useful to organize it into scrapbooks and multiple photo albums. Documentation itself can need a considerably large amount of storage space with census records, copies of original documents and research notebooks.

Chapter 9
"Trouble Getting Started"

Help Finding Names

The most common problem with names in genealogy is finding an ancestor's maiden name. Maiden names tend to be more difficult because the bride traditionally takes on the husband's surname at marriage. However, maiden names can be recovered from documents that record the name of the father. Usually, this problem is resolved from the information on the ancestor's own death certificate.

I was able to obtain the death certificate of my ancestor, Caroline Cross, from the information of her burial in an unmarked grave on record at the garage of the Coloma cemetery. I recovered her maiden name from the document's record of the father, Louis S Pauling.(27) This recovery was especially important because her maiden name was believed to have been *Baldwin* through decades of mispronunciation.

The disadvantage of using the information on an ancestor's death certificate is that it is partially based on the knowledge of an informant. The informant may not know the name of the father or may only know his first name. The informant may also rely on the parental information from a legal perspective, such as in the case of an adoption or legal guardian.

Helpful Tip # 33 Look at Records of Children

Maiden names can often be recovered from documents of an ancestor's children that have recorded the mother's maiden name. This information can usually be found on a child's birth certificate or marriage license. A child's death certificate may also be helpful, especially if the child's death occurred at a very young age.

The name of a bride can be mistaken as a maiden name when there has been a previous marriage. An obvious example of this is when my ancestor married her brother-in-law, as was custom in some areas. The John L DuBreuil's marriage license lists the bride as Mrs Elizabeth DuBreuil. (28) A less obvious example is Albert W Holmer's marriage certificate, which uses the name Rhama Huskey with no indication of her previous marriage that gave her that surname.(29)

Another common problem in genealogy is when the names are changed by the families themselves. Sometimes, the name change can be easily figured out. (An example of this is when the Bauersachs changed their name to Bauersax and then to Bowersox.) Other times, the name change can be very difficult to figure out. For example, I researched multiple census records to discover that Bruno Jasinski changed his family's surname to Daniel.

Helpful Tip # 34 Read Legal Papers

Reading my grandpa's legal papers helped me find the married name of an ancestor. I was having trouble finding a female relative after she had gotten married. The only information I had was from census records, listing her by her maiden name, Alida Holmer. Then, I came across two letters from an attorney for the estate of Alida Henschen, listing my grandfather as an heir.

Helpful Tip # 35 Check Funeral Registers

Checking out my grandparent's funeral register helped me find the first name of an ancestor. I was having trouble finding the correct name for a relative's father. The only information I had was the surname, Leggett, used as her maiden name. Then, I started going through funeral registers and came across the signature of Fred Leggett, whom attended the same funeral as his daughter and son-in-law.

Help Finding Cemeteries

The most common problem with cemeteries in genealogy is finding an ancestor's family cemetery location. Cemetery locations tend to be more difficult to find after a long period of infrequent visitation and lack of use. However, locations can be recovered from documents that record burial information. Usually, this problem is resolved from the information on the ancestor's death certificate.

I was able to obtain the death certificate of my ancestor, Austin Holmer, at the Indiana Department of Health in the city of Gary where he had lived. I recovered the cemetery name, Calumet Park of Gary, from the document's burial information.(30) This recovery was important because the boundaries between the cities of Gary and Merrillville have changed over the decades.

The disadvantage of using the information on an ancestor's death certificate is that it is partially based on the knowledge of an informant. The informant may not know the burial information. Another disadvantage is that older death certificates only recorded minimal information. For example, the death certificate of my ancestor, William DuBreuil, only recorded the place of burial being in Thornton, Illinois.(31)

Helpful Tip # 36 Go to the Township Hall

Information about cemeteries and the directions to get to the location of these cemeteries can be found at the township hall or local government building. The township hall can also give you information on the cemetery sexton, who is actually the person in charge of cemetery records. There may be information on local genealogy and historical societies on hand, too.

Cemetery locations can often be recovered from documents of an ancestor's spouse that have recorded burial information. For example, the family cemetery location for Cedar Park Cemetery in Calumet Park was recovered from the death certificate of the spouse of my great-great uncle, Arthur V Holmer.(32) Another example, the location of the family cemetery in Rapid City, where my uncle was buried, was recovered when I visited for the funeral of my aunt.(33)

Another common problem in genealogy is when the name of a cemetery or location gets changed. Sometimes, the location can easily be figured out. (The Fremont Holbrook cemetery, now owned and operated under a different name, is an example of this.) Other times, a cemetery change can be very difficult to figure out. For example, the Old Church cemetery in Centreville was moved in town to another location and four graves are still missing.

Helpful Tip # 37 Visit the Sheriff

Visiting the Sheriff helped me find a cemetery location. I was having trouble finding the location of a family cemetery within a specific township. The only information I had was the township name, Sherman. Then, I visited the Sheriff's office and was able to look at their enlarged platte map of the area and came across the cemetery hidden behind the old Lutheran church.

Helpful Tip # 38 See the Clergy

Seeing the clergy helped me find a cemetery location. I was having trouble finding the location of a family cemetery within a small town. The only information I had was that it was in the small town of Radon. Then, I saw a member of the clergy and was able to get directions to the church's cemetery, which was hidden down a long, dead end road leading out of town.

Helpful Tip # 39 Ask the Locals

Asking the locals helped me find a cemetery location. I was having trouble finding the location of a family cemetery that was just outside of town. The only information I had was the name of the town, Alhambra. Then, I asked one of the locals, whose mother was actually buried in the same cemetery, who gave me directions how to best get to the cemetery.

Help Finding Dates

The most common problem with dates in genealogy is finding an ancestor's date of birth. Dates of birth tend to be more difficult in finding because birth records are traditionally the most protected and private of records. However, birth dates can be recovered from documents that record the person's age. Usually, this problem is resolved from the information on the ancestor's tombstone.

I was able to visit the tombstone of my ancestor, Mary Kloko, from the information at an interview about the family cemetery in Centreville. I recovered her date of birth by subtracting her age (65yr, 1mo, 14dy) from her date of death: July 11, 1883. To calculate the birth date, you start by subtracting the day(s). For example, July 11 minus 14 days equals June 27 because there are 30 days in June. To finish calculating, you subtract the month(s) next followed by the years. So, Mary Kloko was born on May 27, 1818.(34)

Helpful Tip # 40 Check Out the SSDI

The Social Security Death Index is a database containing a large percentage of deaths in the United States, over the age of 65, from 1940 to the present. Although the database returns only partial dates of death for some of the earlier records, most all records include the full date of birth. The database can be searched online at ssdi.rootsweb.ancestry. com.

Birth dates can also be recovered from from the information on an ancestor's death certificate. I was able to obtain the death certificate of my ancestor, James Briggs, from libers at the county clerk of the location on his census records. I recovered his date of birth by subtracting his age (79yr, 8mo, 2dy) from his date of death: April 27, 1911. For example, April minus 8 months equals August of the previous year. So, James Briggs was born on August 25, 1831.(35)

The disadvantage of using the information on an ancestor's death certificate is that it is partially based on the knowledge of an informant. The informant may only know the age in years or may not even know the age at all. The informant may also approximate the age based on different factors. For example, the age on the death certificate of my ancestor, Malgorzata Szczesniak, reads: Abt 53 years.(36)

Helpful Tip # 41 Search the Dibean Marriages

A great source of FREE information, for those who have roots in Michigan, is the index of Dibean Marriages. This is a database containing a large number of marriage records in Michigan. Although the database is searchable by counties, the navigation becomes trickier as the database increases in size. It is smart to keep in mind that larger files (354 K) contain more records than smaller files (15 K). The database can be searched online at www.mifamilyhistory.org/dibeanindex/default.asp

Birth dates can also be recovered from the information on an ancestor's marriage license. I was able to obtain the marriage license of my ancestors, Eugene Cross and Charlotte Briggs, from the information in the dibean index. I recovered an approximate date of birth for each by subracting their age at the time of marriage (23 and 18) from the marriage date: December 8, 1878. So, Eugene Cross was born abt 1855 and Charlotte Briggs was born abt 1860.(37)

Remember

Don't forget to update your ancestor chart, filling in dates and any new names that you might have come across from all of your research. The further back you research, the more ancestors there are per generation. After researching, my chart now looks something like this:

(Seventh Generation)
88 Enoch Cross
89 Polly Loy (1798-?)
90 Louis S Pauling
104 George Leggett
105 Mary Leggett
106 Zebulon Barnes
107 Mary Woolever
108 Jacob Reinke
109 Caroline Lipke (1811-1910)
110 Martin Able
112 Christopher Kloko
113 Maria Hall (1789-1855)
120 John Bauersax (1799-1881)
121 Magdalena Walter (1800-1853)
122 Christian Kerr (1800-?)
123 Mary A Kerr (1805-?)
124 Isaac Boudeman (1804-1894)
125 Susan Fortner (1807-1871)
126 John Seas (1807-1880)
127 Lydia Haberling (1812-1892)

(Eighth Generation)
240 George Adam Bauersachs (1774-?)
241 Mary Steinbrook (1776-1860)
244 Jacob Kerr
250 John Fortner
251 Elizabeth Fortner
252 George Seas
253 Elizabeth Seas

Chapter 10
"Trouble With Accuracy"

Conflicting Information

One of the biggest obstacles in genealogy is when you have conflicting information, a discrepency between different sources for the same data. Conflicting information usually results from either incorrect information obtained without verification or information compiled or copied incorrectly. Generally, original records written at or closer to the event in question are most accurate. However, the preponderance of information may help decide when there are no original records.

When I went to visit the grave of my ancestor, Malgorzata Szczesniak, I recorded the dates on her tombstone: 1869-1930.(38) From this information, I was able to obtain her death certificate, which listed her age as: Abt 53.(39) However, Fifty-three years of age would place her birth in 1877--eight years later. There was also a discrepency in her age, 19, recorded on the 1892 marriage license, which would place her birth in 1873.(40) Unfortunately, I was unable to obtain any birth record or original document.

The death certificate, which also states that the date of birth was unknown, used unverified information from the informant, Wojciech Szczesniak, for the recorded age. Although the marriage license was written closer to the time of birth, I searched through the census records to create a preponderance of information. The 1900-1930 censuses recorded her age as 28, 37, 48 and 60, respectively.

(41,42,9,43) And, even though the census records had discrepencies themselves, they helped me make the decision to use 1873 as her birth year.

Helpful Tip # 42 Birthdays and Anniversaries

Because birthdays and anniversaries are celebrated every year, their impact on the memory is usually more vivid than other memories. The information about them tends to be more accurate, especially by those who have participated in their celebrations. Also, the month and day of an occassion is remembered more accurately than the year in which the event began.

Accuracy in Births

When deciding between conflicting information, the most accurate information about births are original records that were written at or near the time of birth. These records may include an actual birth certificate or records obtained from county clerks that are exact duplicates of the actual birth record. Other original documents include christening and baptismal records. Birth dates that occur after christening or baptismal records are either incorrect or records pertaining to different individuals.

When original documentation is missing, more accurate information about births can be found on original records closer to the time of birth. These records may include confirmation, bar/bat mitzvah and marriage records, especially if the event has religious ties to the actual age of the individual. Copies of records that are exact duplicates are also considered more accurate.

Compilation records are usually next in the order of accuracy when deciding between conflicting information.

These records include birth records obtained from county clerks that are copied from a liber, birth liber records, birth indexes, marriage records obtained from county clerks that are copied from a liber, marriage liber records, marriage indexes and church records.

The least accurate information about births, in order starting with the most reliable, are: original death records or records obtained from the county clerk that are exact duplicates of the actual death record, records obtained from the county clerk that are copied from a liber, death liber records, cemetery records, and dates on tombstones. Finally, census records are not reliable for births; however, they are better than having no information at all.

Helpful Tip # 43 Read Postcards & Letters

Accurate dates can be found from reading postcards or letters. I found the birthdate of my great grandpa from reading a post card that gave details of their vacation.(44) In another card, I found information about their marriage when they were celebrating their 25th anniversary.(45) Reading the letters or cards can often times give you enough information for discerning exact dates.

Accuracy in Deaths

When deciding between conflicting information, the most accurate information about deaths are original records that were written at or near the time of death. These records may include an actual death certificate or records obtained from county clerks that are exact duplicates of the actual death record. Cemetery or burial records are also very accurate. Dates of death that occur after burial records are either incorrect or records pertaining to different individuals.

Compilation records are usually next in the order of accuracy when deciding between conflicting information. These records include death records obtained from county clerks that are copied from a liber, death liber records, death indexes and church records. Finally, dates on tombstones are also usually reliable for deaths; however, markers and replacement stones made later on are unreliable.

Helpful Tip # 44 Name Abbreviations
Some names are written in an abbreviated form. For example, McDonald is the abbreviated form for MacDonald. Search engines and indexes that are based on an alphabetical order can place these names in a different order that expected. Accordingly, most indexes will place these names in this order: Mabel, McDonald, Masters and Matthewson.

Misinterpreted Handwriting
Another common problem with accuracy in genealogy is misinterpreted handwriting. Handwriting is usually misinterpreted because the mind often times sees what it wants to see, especially if it is crossed, written with a flag or written too sloppily. Computer programs can also make mistakes like reading a crease in the paper as a line or a smudge as a mark. However, these conflicts can be resolved when the interpreter has other outside knowledge, like what the correct character should be.

Correct:	Commonly mistaken for:
0	6,8
1	6,7,9
2	3,5
3	2,5

4	1,7,9,11
5	2,3
6	0,1
7	1,4,9
8	0,9
9	0,1
a	c,e,h,n,o,q
b	h
c	a,e,o
d	s
e	a,c,i,l,o,t
h	a,b,k,tt
i	e,j,o
j	i
k	h
l	e,r
m	n,ni
n	a,m,r,u,v,w,x
o	a,c,e,i,s,u
p	y
q	a
r	l,n,s
s	b,c,e,d,o,r
t	e
u	ar,ei,n,o,rs,v,w
v	n,u
w	n,u,z
x	n,y
y	ij,p,x
z	w

Chapter 11
"Putting It All Together"

Numbering Systems

When it comes to putting it all together for publishing, there are many different numbering systems for genealogists to choose from. The numbering system is used because of its ease in understanding relations between descendants without the repetition of words. However, there seems to be no standardization between which system to use. I, in fact, have created my own system for numbering by finding out what works best for me.

Register System

Register is a descending numbering system. It begins with the Progenitor, uses both common and Roman numerals and can usually be recognized by only children with a progeny being assigned a common numeral. It only counts the children, with only those having a progeny being recorded in the suceeding generation. It also counts the earliest generation first and follows chronological order.

```
      (-Generation One-)
  1   Progenitor
      2   i   Descendant

      (-Generation Two-)
  2   Descendant
      3    i   Descendant's Progeny
          ii   Descendant's Progeny (no progeny)
      4  iii   Descendant's Progeny
```

The advantages of using this system is that siblings are grouped together. The disadvantages of using this system is that everyone's number changes BOTH for adding a future generation (progeny) and for finding another generation back of ancestors (changing the Progenitor). Another disadvantage is that there are quite a few numerals.

For example:

```
        (-Generation One-)
1   Peter Holmer
    2   i   John Elbert Holmer

        (-Generation Two-)
2   John Elbert Holmer
    3   i   Arthur V Holmer
       ii   Alida Holmer
    4 iii   Austin Walter Holmer

        (-Generation Three-)
3   Arthur V Holmer
        i   Evangeline J Holmer
4   Austin Walter Holmer
    5   i   Arthur Joseph Holmer
    6  ii   Albert Walter Holmer
    7 iii   Lawrence Holmer

        (-Generation Four-)
5   Arthur Joseph Holmer
6   Albert Walter Holmer
7   Lawrence Holmer
```

NGSQ System

NGSC (also known as Record and Modified Register) is a descending numbering system. It begins with the Progenitor, uses both common and Roman numerals and can usually be recognized by all children being assigned a common numeral, but only children with a progeny being marked with a '+' sign. It only counts the children, with only those having a progeny being recorded in the suceeding generation. It also counts the earliest generation first and follows chronological order.

```
     (-Generation One-)
 1  Progenitor
    + 2   i  Descendant

     (-Generation Two-)
 2  Descendant
    + 3   i   Descendant's Progeny
      4  ii   Descendant's Progeny (no progeny)
    + 5 iii   Descendant's Progeny
```

The advantages of using this system is that siblings are grouped together. The disadvantages of using this system is that everyone's number changes BOTH for adding a future generation (progeny) and for finding another generation back of ancestors (changing the Progenitor). Another disadvantage is that there are quite a few numerals and order discontinuity in the suceeding generations where there is no progeny.

For example:

```
     (-Generation One-)
 1  Adalbert Szczesniak
    +  2    i  Walter Szczesniak
    +  3   ii  Mary Szczesniak
    +  4  iii  Helen Irene Szczesniak
    +  5   iv  Martha Szczesniak
    +  6    v  Frances M Szczesniak
    +  7   vi  Wladyshaw Szczesniak
       8  vii  Casimer Szczesniak

     (-Generation Two-)
 2  Walter Szczesniak
       9    i  Clara Szczesniak
      10   ii  Frederick Szczesniak
      11  iii  Edward J Szczesniak
 3  Mary Szczesniak
      12    i  Eugene Dudek
      13   ii  Clara Dudek
      14  iii  Cecilia Dudek
      15   iv  Stanley Dudek Jr.
```

```
4  Helen Irene Szczesniak
   + 16   i   Arthur Joseph Holmer
   + 17  ii   Albert Walter Holmer
   + 18 iii   Lawrence Holmer
5  Martha Szczesniak
     19    i   Dorothy Sieczkowski
     20   ii   Theodore Sieczkowski
     21  iii   Virginia Sieczkowski
     22   iv   Adeline Sieczkowski
     23    v   Irene Sieczkowski
6  Frances M Szczesniak
     24    i   Bruno Jasinski Jr.
7  Wladyshaw Szczesniak
     25    i   Richard Hermanski
     26   ii   Dolores Hermanski

     (-Generation Three-)
16  Arthur Joseph Holmer
17  Albert Walter Holmer
18  Lawrence Holmer
```

Henry System

Henry is a descending numbering system. It begins with the Progenitor, uses characters (digits 1-9, letters X, A-W, Y, Z) and can usually be recognized as an indented list. It only counts the children, with each suceeding generation adding a character to the previous string of characters. It also counts in an order of 1,2,3...9,X,A,B,C...W,Y,Z.

```
1. Progenitor
  11. Descendant
    111. Descendant's Progeny
      1111. Progeny
    112. Descendant's Progeny (no progeny)
    113. Descendant's Progeny
      1131. Progeny
```

The advantages of using this system is that the list eliminates redundancy and adding a future generation (progeny) doesn't change everyone's number. The disadvantage to using this system is that there is a ridiculously long string of numerals and everyone's number changes everytime you add an ancestor (change Progenitor). For example:

```
1. Augustus DuBreuil
   11. William A DuBreuil
      111. Loa E DuBreuil
      112. Genevieve B DuBreuil
      113. Weldon B DuBreuil
      114. Allan Louis DuBreuil
         1141. Rhama Alene DuBreuil
            11411. Eugene Warren Huskey
      115. Forest F DuBreuil
      116. Winfield R DuBreuil
         1161. Loa DuBreuil
      117. Beane DuBreuil
   12. John L DuBreuil
   13. John DuBreuil
   14. Hattie E DuBreuil
   15. Edwin DuBreuil
      151. Russell H DuBreuil
```

Modified Henry System

Modified Henry is a descending system. It begins with the Progenitor, uses common numerals and can usually be recognized as an indented list. It only counts the children, with each suceeding generation adding a numeral to the previous string of numerals. It also counts in an order of 1,2,3...9,(10),(11),(12), etc.

```
1. Progenitor
   11. Descendant
      111. Descendant's Progeny
         1111. Progeny
      112. Descendant's Progeny (no progeny)
      113. Descendant's Progeny
         1131. Progeny
```

The advantages of using this system is that the list eliminates redundancy and adding a future generation (progeny) doesn't change everyone's number. The disadvantage to using this system is that there is a ridiculously long string of numerals and everyone's number changes everytime you add an ancestor (change Progenitor). For example:

```
1. Enoch Cross
   11. Wesley Cross
      111. Alpheus Cross
         1111. Claude Cross
         1112. Maude Cross
      112. George Cross
      113. William Cross
      114. Eugene Cross
         1141. Alberta Cross
         1142. Roy Cross
         1143. May Cross
         1144. Myrtle Cross
            11441. Rhama DuBreuil
               114411. Eugene Huskey
      115. Ceylon Cross
      116. Mary Cross
         1161. Fred Swails
         1162. Ed Swails
   12. Albert Cross
      121. Alonzo Cross
      122. Nelson Cross
      123. Enoch Cross
      124. Emogene Cross
   13. Abner Cross
      131. Alice Cross
      132. Charles Cross
   14. Samuel Cross
      141. Alpheus Cross
      142. Edwin Cross
   15. Enoch Cross
      151. Dora Cross
      152. Percy Cross
      153. Floyd Cross
      154. Walter Cross
      155. Harriet Cross
   16. Eliza Cross
      161. Julia Cross
```

d'Aboville System

D'Aboville is a descending numbering system. It begins with the Progenitor, uses common numerals seperated by periods and can usually be recognized as an indented list. It only counts the children, with each suceeding generation adding a numeral to the previous string of numerals.

```
1 Progenitor
  1.1 Descendant
    1.1.1 Descendant's Progeny
      1.1.1.1 Progeny
    1.1.2 Descendant's Progeny (no progeny)
    1.1.3 Descendant's Progeny

      1.1.3.1 Progeny
```

The advantages of using this system is that the list eliminates redundancy and adding a future generation (progeny) doesn't change everyone's number. The disadvantage to using this system is that there is a ridiculously long string of numerals and everyone's number changes everytime you add an ancestor (change Progenitor). For example:

```
1 Eliza Reed
  1.1 Mary Reed
  1.2 Abel W Reed
    1.2.1 Jennie E Reed
    1.2.2 Delila C Reed
    1.2.3 Ezra H Reed
      1.2.3.1 Jennie Reed
      1.2.3.2 Nettie Reed
      1.2.3.3 Abel Reed
      1.2.3.4 William Reed
        1.2.3.4.1 Kathryn Reed
        1.2.3.4.2 Virginia Reed
        1.2.3.4.3 Martha Reed
        1.2.3.4.4 William Reed
        1.2.3.4.5 Frederick Reed
        1.2.3.4.6 Kenneth Reed
      1.2.3.5 Philetus Reed
```

```
1.2.3.6 Charles P Reed
  1.2.3.6.1 Dgola Reed
  1.2.3.6.2 Grace Reed
  1.2.3.6.3 Jennie Reed
  1.2.3.6.4 Robert Reed
  1.2.3.6.5 Elize Reed
1.2.3.7 Walter Reed
1.2.3.8 Mamie Reed
1.2.3.9 Edith T Reed
1.2.4 Empson L Reed
1.2.5 Mary Jane Reed
1.2.6 Philander S Reed
1.3 Jacob Reed
1.3.1 Sarah Reed
```

Meurgey de Tupigny System

Meurgey de Tupigny is a descending system. It begins
with the Progenitor, uses both Roman and common numerals
and can usually be recognized as an indented list. It only
counts the children, assigning a Roman numeral (for
generation) and a common numeral (for children order)
seperated by a hyphen.

```
I Progenitor
  II-1 Descendant
    III-1 Descendant's Progeny
      IV-1 Progeny
    III-2 Descendant's Progeny (no progeny)
    III-3 Descendant's Progeny
      IV-1 Progeny
```

The advantages of using this system is that the list
eliminates redundancy and adding a future generation
(progeny) doesn't change everyone's number. The
disadvantage to using this system is that there are quite a few
numerals and everyone's number changes everytime you add
an ancestor (change Progenitor).

For example:

```
I George H Leggett
  II-1 William H Leggett
  II-2 Mary J Leggett
  II-3 Bersheba Leggett
  II-4 Jesse G Leggett
    III-1 Mary E Leggett
    III-2 William Leggett
    III-3 Sarah Leggett
    III-4 Alexander Leggett
    III-5 Frederick Leggett
      IV-1 Bernice Leggett
      IV-2 Josephine Esther Leggett
        V-1 William Reed Jr.
        V-2 Frederick Reed
        V-3 Kenneth Frederick Reed
      IV-3 Victor Leggett
      IV-4 Myrtle Leggett
      IV-5 Mary Leggett
    III-6 Jesse G Leggett Jr.
  II-5 Richard Leggett
  II-6 Samantha Leggett
```

de Villiers/Pama System

De Villiers/Pama is a descending system. It begins with a Progenitor, uses both letters and common numerals and can usually be recognized as an indented list. It only counts the children, assigning a letter (for generation) and a common numeral (for children order).

```
a Progenitor
  b1 Descendant
    c1 Descendant's Progeny
      d1 Progeny
    c2 Descendant's Progeny (no progeny)
    c3 Descendant's Progeny
      d1 Progeny
```

The advantages of using this system is that the list eliminates redundancy, adding a future generation (progeny) doesn't change everyone's number, and the assigned number is minimal. The disadvantage to using this system is that

somewhat difficult to read and everyone's number changes everytime you add an ancestor (change Progenitor).
For example:

```
a Christopher Kloko
  b1 George Kloko
     c1 Christian C Kloko
        d1 Henry W Kloko
           e1 Richard H Kloko
        d2 Frank E Kloko
        d3 Clarence F Kloko
           e1 Harold Kloko
        d4 Lawrence F Kloko
           e1 Donald Kloko
  b2 Frederick Kloko
     c1 Herman Frederick Kloko
        d1 Edward F Kloko
        d2 Edith M Kloko
           e1 Howard Kramer
           e2 Lawrence Kramer
           e3 Edna Lucille Kramer
        d3 Ella Edith Kloko
           e1 James E Hazel
        d4 Edna E Kloko
           e1 Doris Irene Depue
           e2 Harold Eugene DePue
        d5 Ervin Louis Kloko
           e1 Kenneth Carol Kloko
           e2 Dale Richard Kloko
           e3 Beulah Carolyn Kloko
           e4 Wesley Ervin Kloko
           e5 Doris Arlene Kloko
           e6 Paul Keith Kloko
           e7 Mary Kloko
```

Holmer (my own) System

Holmer is a descending system. It begins with a Progenitor, uses characters (digits 1-9, letters A-Z) and can usually be recognized as an indented list. It only counts the children, assigning a character (for generation) and a character (for children order) seperated by a period. It also counts in an order of 1,2,3...9,A,B,C...X,Y,Z.

```
1.0 Progenitor
  2.1 Descendant
    3.1 Descendnat's Progeny
      4.1 Progeny
    3.2 Descendant's Progeny (no progeny)
    3.3 Descendant's Progeny
      4.1 Progeny
```

I created this system by discarding what I didn't like and using what I did like from each of the previous numbering systems. Using indentation to organize the list by generations, I eliminated the redundancy in Register and NGSQ; and, at the same time, eliminated the excessive string of numerals in Henry, Modified Henry, and d'Aboville. By adapting the counting sequence from Henry, moving the 'X' back in its place, I eliminated the large amount of Roman numerals in Meurgey de Tupigny and the difficult read in de Villiers/Pama.

For example:

```
1.0 George Adam Bauersachs
  2.1 John Bauersax
    3.1 Jacob J Bowersox
      4.1 Ezra E Bowersox
        5.1 Lloyd F Bowersox
        5.2 Margret H Bowersox
        5.3 Ila M Bowersox
      4.2 Cloid Bowersox
      4.3 Clarence Bowersox
      4.4 Carrie Belle Bowersox
      4.5 Edna Bowersox
      4.6 Florence Bowersox
      4.7 Milroy Bowersox
    3.2 Solomon J Bowersox
      4.1 Joanna Bowersox
      4.2 Martin Theodore Bowersox
        5.1 Earl E Bowersox
          6.1 Gerald Bowersox
          6.2 Mary Jeannette Bowersox
        5.2 Hazel B Bowersox
      4.3 Robert B Bowersox
```

```
5.1 Pearl Bowersox
5.2 Raymond Bowersox
   6.1 Betty J Bowersox
   6.2 Raymond Bowersox Jr
   6.3 Billie Bowersox
5.3 Irene Bowersox
5.4 Leila Bowersox
5.5 Evelyn Bowersox
5.6 Walter Bowersox
5.7 LeRoy Bowersox
4.4 Allen Bowersox
5.1 Ethel Marie Bowersox
   6.1 Allen Marcus Lewis
   6.2 June Lewis
   6.3 Robert John Lewis
   6.4 Elsie Marie Lewis
   6.5 Harriet Ethel Lewis
   6.6 Harry Vern Lewis
   6.7 Galien Carl Lewis
5.2 Bernice Olive Bowersox
   6.1 Kenneth Carol Kloko
   6.2 Dale Richard Kloko
   6.3 Beulah Carolyn Kloko
   6.4 Wesley Ervin Kloko
   6.5 Doris Arlene Kloko
   6.6 Paul Keith Kloko
   6.7 Mary Kloko
5.3 Helen Myra Bowersox
   6.1 Bernice Weinberg
   6.2 Willis Weinberg Jr.
5.4 Lucille Bowersox
5.5 Ruth May Bowersox
   6.1 Ramona Mae Miller
   6.2 Ralph Dean Miller
   6.3 Richard Allen Miller
   6.4 Jack Edward MIller
   6.5 George LaVern Miller
   6.6 Shirley Ann Miller
   6.7 Thomas Owen Miller
5.6 Russell Allen Bowesox
4.5 Rosa May Bowersox
4.6 Charity Bowersox
4.7 Vera Bowersox
4.8 Frederick A Bowersox
4.9 Ida M Bowersox
4.A Reva I Bowersox
```

Remember

Final reminder. Be careful publishing information about living persons! Some genealogy computer programs will automatically do this for you by publishing the person as *Living Holmer* with masked birth and marriage information until some death information is entered.

Appendices

Appendix A:
List of Surnames

For centuries, cultures have been using surnames as a means to record their genealogy. "Holmer" was first used as a surname by my family in the 1800s. It was given to my ancestors because they came from Stockholm. Other surnames used by my family have been traced back as far as the mid-1600s and have also been given to my ancestors because of their occupation, like "Bauman" for woodsmen, or their association with land features, like "Reed".

Abbett ABBOTT; Abel, ABLE; ALDRICH; ANDERSON, Enderson;

BARBER; BARCZAK; BARNARD; BARNES, Bunce; BAUMAN, Baumen, Bouman, Bowman; BECHT; BECK; Badman, Baudeman, Bodman, Bondaman, Bondman, Boodman, Borsdenian, BOUDEMAN, Boudman, Bowdman, Buddman, Budman; Bauersachs, Bauersax, Bowcroux, Bowersock, Bowersocks, Bowerson, Bowersoy, BOWERSOX; BRIGGS; BROWN;

CLARK; Cobb, Crab, Crass, CROSS, Crob, Crow;

DANIEL; DePUE; DOMINIAK, Dominick; DREIBELBIS; Dubrenil, DuBreuell, DuBREUIL, DuBreuill, DuBreuit, DuBrevil, DuBriell, DuBrill, DuBriul; DUDEK;

ENOS;

FORTNER, Fostner;

GARCEAU;

Haberlin, HABERLING, Heberlin, Heberling; Hale, HALL, Halt, Hole, Holl, Holt; Harten, HARTER, Hartes, Haster, Hesten, Hester; HARWOOD; HAZEL; HENDERSHOT; Hensan, HENSCHEN, Henshen, Herschen; HERMANSKI; HERSON; Holbrock, HOLBROOK; Hobner, Hohner, HOLMER, Homar; HUSKEY;

JACKSON; JASINSKI; JONES;

KERR; Kasko, Klocke, Kloka, Kloke, KLOKO, Klokow, Kloks, Kolke; KOONS; Kramar, KRAMER; Kub, KUSS;

LANCASTER; LANE; LAZEAR; Legate, Leget, Leggate, Leggatt, Legget, LEGGETT, Leggitt, Liggett; LEWIS; LIPKE; LORING; Lay, LOY;

MCCAULEY; MCDONALD; MACDONALD; MANN;

PAULING; PFAUTH; POLMANTEER;

RAYMOND; REED, Reid, Ried; Ranke, REINKE, Renkie, Runke;

SADOWSKI; Seace, SEAS; SHISLEY; SIECZKOWSKI; SMITH; Strie, STRY; Swaile, Swailes, SWAILS, Swales; Szazniak, Szcesniak, SZCZESNIAK;

WALDRON; WOOLEVER;

YOUSON;

Appendix B:
Works Cited

One of the most important lessons pertaining to any education is giving credit where credit is due. This section is reserved for my Works Cited page, and a very useful tool for others to search for their own genealogy!

(1) Holmer, Donna. Interview. October 2002.
(2) Holmer, Albert Sr. Interview. November 2002.
(3) Holmer Tombstone. Coloma Cemetery. June 2010.
(4) 1930 Census Index. Ancestry.com. September 2010.
(5) 1920 Census Index. Ancestry.com. September 2010.
(6) Herman Kloko household. US Federal Census. 1900.
(7) Christian Kloko household. US Federal Census. 1900.
(8) Walter Holmer household. US Federal Census. 1920.
(9) Wojcich Szczesniak household. US Federal Census. 1920.
(10) Warren Huskey household. US Federal Census. 1930.
(11) William Reed household. US Federal Census. 1930.
(12) Wesley Cross household. US Federal Census. 1850.
(13) Abner Cross household. US Federal Census. 1850.
(14) Wesley Cross household. US Federal Census. 1870.
(15) "Public Inspection of Vital Records for Genealogical Purposes at the Berrien County Clerk's Office". Berrien County Clerk. 2007.
(16) "Tina Leary Van Buren County Clerk". Van Buren County Clerk. 2006.
(17) "Linda Coburn Grand Traverse County Clerk: Genealogical Resources". Grand Traverse County Clerk. December 2005.

(18) "Death Index 1867-1929". St. Joseph County Clerk. 2006.

(19) "Liber 1 Death Records 1867-1892". St. Joseph County Clerk. 2006.

(20) "Liber 2 Death Records 1893-1912". St. Joseph County Clerk. 2006.

(21) Archives. theH-P.com. January 2011.

(22) "Doris Kloko and William Reed Are Wed in Home Rites". Niles Daily Star.

(23) "Files For Divorce". Niles Daily Star.

(24) "Infant Rites". Niles Daily Star.

(25) "Mrs. Wilhelmina Kloko". Three Rivers Commercial News.

(26) "Catholic Prayer Cards." Aquinasandmore.com. October 5, 2010.

(27) Record D-143. Caroline Cross Death Certificate. February 1, 1915.

(28) Record 27444. DuBreuil marriage license. August 5, 1876.

(29) Holmer Marriage Certificate. original. December 26, 1939.

(30) Record 67-1376. Austin Holmer Death Certificate. October 10, 1967.

(31) Record 31562. William DuBreuil Certificate of Death. November 16, 1916.

(32) Record 01653. Ella Holmer Certificate of Death. March 11, 1977.

(33) Graveside Services. Frances Huskey memory folder. May 21, 2007.

(34) Kloko Tombstone. Prairie River Cemetery. December 2010.

(35) Record 74. James Briggs Certified Copy Record of Death. May 20, 1911.

(36) Record 19020. Malgorzata Szczesniak Certificate of Death. July 7, 1930.

(37) Record 50. Cross Certified Copy of Record of Marriage. December 8, 1878.

(38) Szczesniak Tombstone. Holy Cross Cemetery. May 2007.

(39) Record 19020. Malgorzata Szczesniak Certificate of Death. July 7, 1930.

(40) Record 191175. Szczesniak Marriage License. November 15, 1892.

(41) Adalbert Szczesniak household. US Federal Census. 1900.

(42) Wojciech Szczesniak household. US Federal Census. 1910.

(43) Albert Szczesniak household. US Federal Census. 1930.

(44) Beautiful Fall Colors in the Rockies. Rawlins, WY postcard. July 18, 1960.

(45) Dubuque, Iowa. Decorah, IA postcard. June 29, 1960.

Appendix C:
Tombstone Transcriptions

Bakertown Cemetery, Buchanan, MI
Directions: From US31, exit at US12 (exit 3) and travel west 4.0 miles to Bakertown Road. Turn north onto Bakertown and travel 1.5 miles to Galien Buchanan Road. Turn west onto Galien Buchanan and travel 0.75 mile to Hess Road. Turn onto Hess and cemetery entrance on the west side of the road.

```
-------------
|  GRANDMA  |
|   REINKE  |
| 1818-1911 |
-------------
```

Beard Cemetery, Leonidas, MI
Directions: From Interstate 94, exit at US131 (exit 74A) and travel south 13.5 miles to Michigan. Turn east onto Michigan and travel 13 miles to N. Summit Rd. Turn north onto Summit and travel 2 miles to the cemetery entrance on the west side of the road.

```
-----------------------------------
|   LYDIA SEAS         JOHN SEAS    |
| Born AUG 10 1812   Born OCT 25 1807 |
| Died OCT 10 1892   Died OCT 25 1880 |
-----------------------------------
```

```
-------------------
| WILLIAM H SEAS  |
|    1840-1926    |
-------------------
```

```
      --------
      | SEAS |
      --------


---------------    -------------
| PETER SEAS |    |   MARY A  |
| 1843-1920  |    | His Wife  |
--------------    | 1866-1955 |
                  -------------


      -------------
      |   LENA    |
      | Daughter  |
      | 1893-1951 |

      -------------
```

Burr Oak Township Cemetery, Burr Oak, MI

Directions: From US12, turn north onto Halfway Road (CR148) and travel 1.7 miles to West Front Street. Turn west onto Front and travel 0.5 mile to Middle Colon Road. Turn north onto Middle Colon and travel 0.2 mile to cemetery entrance on the west side of the road.

```
---------------------------
|        STEVEN   C        |
|        LANCASTER         |
| Sept 16 1951-Oct 20 1978 |
---------------------------
```

Calumet Park, Gary, IN

Directions: From Interstate 80/94, exit at I-53 (exit 10) and travel south 2.75 miles to US30. Turn west onto US30 and travel .6 miles to the cemetery entrance on the north side of the road.

```
-------------------    -------------------
| Beloved Husband |    |  Beloved Wife   |
|  AUSTIN WALTER  |    | HELEN ELIZABETH |
|     HOLMER      |    |     HOLMER      |
| July 18   Oct 4 |    | Mar 26   Mar 18 |
|   1893     1967 |    |  1906     1971  |
-------------------    -------------------
```

Cedar Park Cemetery, Calumet Park, IL
Directions: From Interstate 57, exit at 127th Street (exit 353) and travel east 1.0 mile to Halsted Street. Turn north onto Halsted and travel .1 mile to the cemetery entrance on the west side of the road.

```
 ----------------    --------------------
|    Mother     |   |      Father        |
|  ELLA HOLMER  |   |  ARTHUR V HOLMER   |
|   1893 1977   |   |   1889      1955   |
 ----------------    --------------------

        -----------------------
       |       Daughter        |
       |  EVANGELINE J HOLMER  |
       |   1916          1972  |
        -----------------------
```

Coloma Cemetery, Coloma, MI
Directions: From Interstate 196 (US31), exit at Coloma Road (exit 4) and travel east 3.5 miles to the cemetery entrance on the south side of the road.

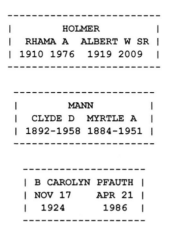

```
        -------------------------
       |         HOLMER          |
       |  RHAMA A   ALBERT W SR  |
       |  1910 1976  1919 2009   |
        -------------------------

        -----------------------
       |         MANN          |
       |  CLYDE D   MYRTLE A    |
       |  1892-1958 1884-1951   |
        -----------------------

        --------------------
       |  B CAROLYN PFAUTH  |
       |  NOV 17     APR 21 |
       |   1924        1986 |
        --------------------
```

Fairview Memorial Cemetery, Watervliet, MI

Directions: From Interstate 94, exit at M-140 (exit 41) and travel north .5 miles to Red Arrow highway. Turn east onto Red Arrow and travel 2.0 miles to the cemetery entrance on the north side of the road.

```
-----------------------------
|         McDONALD          |
|   GORDON J      DORIS A   |
| June 20 1934  Nov  9 1931 |
|               Nov 16 1995 |
-----------------------------
```

Holy Cross Cemetery, Calumet City, IL

Directions: From Interstate 94/80, exit at US-41 North Calumet Avenue (exit 1) and travel north 1.5 miles to 165th Street. Turn west onto 165th and travel 1.0 mile to the state line. Continue west on River Oak Drive 1.0 mile to Burnham Avenue. Turn north onto Burnham and travel .2 mile to Michigan City Road. Turn west onto Michigan City and travel .2 mile to cemetery entrance on the south side of the road.

```
--------------   --------------
|   Ojciec   |   |   Matha    |
|  WOJCIECH  |   | MALGORZATA |
| SZCZESNIAK |   | SZCZESNIAK |
| 1873  1947 |   | 1869  1930 |
--------------   --------------

--------------   --------------
|   Father   |   |   Mother   |
|   WALTER   |   |   BERTHA   |
| SZCZESNIAK |   | SZCZESNIAK |
| 1893  1964 |   | 1895  1962 |
--------------   --------------
```

```
 --------------       --------------
|   Father    |     |   Mother    |
|   WALTER    |     |   MARTHA    |
| SIECKOWSKI  |     | SIECKOWSKI  |
| 1894  1957  |     | 1899  1972  |
 --------------       --------------


  -------------       -------------
 | WLADYSHAW  |     |  SYLVESTER |
 | HERMANSKI  |     |  HERMANSKI |
 | 1904 1971  |     |  1902 1984 |
  -------------       -------------


 ----------------------       ----------------------
|       Mother         |     |       Father         |
|  SYLVIA  SZCZESNIAK  |     | CASIMER  SZCZESNIAK  |
|   1907       1964    |     |  1907        1974    |
 ----------------------       ----------------------


          -------------------
         |   Wife, Mom       |
         |   and Granny      |
         | DOLORES BARCZAK   |
         |   1926 - 1995     |
          -------------------
```

Homewood Memorial Gardens (formerly, Fremont
Holbrook Cemetery), Homewood, IL
    Directions: From Interstate 94, exit at Torrence Avenue
(exit 161) and travel south .6 miles to Thornton-Lansing
Road. Turn west onto Thornton-Lansing and travel 3.4 miles
to Ridge Road. Turn south onto Ridge and travel .5 miles to
the cemetery entrance on the north side of the road.

```
        ------------
       |  HOLBROOK  |
        ------------


  -------------       -------------
 |  MARY E    |     |  JOSEPH R  |
 | 1817-1884  |     | 1814-1881  |
  -------------       -------------
```

109

```
 -------------    -------------
| PHOEBE A  |   |  FREMONT   |
| 1851-1937 |   | 1851-1926  |
 -------------    -------------


        -------------
       |    RAY      |
       |  ROCKWOOD   |
       | 1881-1929   |
        -------------


 -------------------------
|       HOLBROOK          |
|  ANNE R      CLARK      |
| 1837-1899 1838-1904     |
 -------------------------
```

Lakeview Cemetery, South Haven, MI

Directions: From Interstate 196 (US31), exit at North Shore Drive (exit 22) and travel west 0.2 mile to Blue Star Highway (US63). Turn south onto Blue Star and travel 1.5 miles to the cemetery entrance on the west side of the road.

```
 -------------    -----------------------
| ORA CROSS |   | Capt ALONZO BARNEY |
|  HARWOOD  |   |       CROSS           |
| 1887-1978 |   |     1854-1914         |
 -------------    -----------------------


      ----------------------
     | HARRIET MacDONALD    |
     |       CROSS           |
     |     1866-1916         |
      ----------------------


 ----------------------    --------------------
|      HARRIET         |  |       MARY         |
| JACKSON MacDONALD    |  | BA+HATTIE CROSS    |
| Born Feb  17 1830    |  |   May 24 1887      |
| Died Sept 24 1894    |  |   Oct 3   1888     |
 ----------------------    --------------------


           ---------
          | CROSS |
           ---------
```

```
------------- ------------
|  ALBERT J  | | NELSON A |
|   CROSS    | |  -cant-  |
| 1889-1978  | |  -read-  |
------------- ------------


----------------  ---------------------
| ALBERT CROSS |  | JANE HERSON CROSS |
|  1826-1902   |  |     1827-1907     |
----------------  ---------------------


        ---------------
        | ABNER CROSS |
        |     CO1     |
        |  1 MICH CAV |
        ---------------
```

North Shore Memory Gardens, Hagar Shores, MI

Directions: From Interstate 196 (US31), exit at Coloma Road (exit 4) and travel west 2.0 miles to M-63. Turn north onto M-63 and travel 1.5 miles to the cemetery entrance on the west side of the road.

```
----------------------------------
|    ARTHUR J        MARY L       |
|  May 22 1917    August 26 1923  |
| March 3 1969     June  30 2004  |
|            HOLMER               |
----------------------------------


    ---------------------------
    | KENNETH E Sr     JOAN G |
    |  1931-1990     1951-2003 |
    |           CLARK          |
    ---------------------------


----------------------  --------------------
| KENNETH E CLARK Jr |  | LaDONNA L CLARK |
|  Jun 12   July 17  |  |  1967     1984  |
|   1952      1994   |  |                 |
----------------------  --------------------
```

Oak Ridge Cemetery, Buchanan, MI

Directions: From US31, exit at Buchanan Road (exit 5) and travel west 3.3 miles to cemetery entrance on the south side of the road.

```
-----------------------
|      LEGGETT        |
|  ESTHER L JESSE G Sr |
|  1834-1910 1836-1892 |
|   Mother    Father   |
-----------------------


-----------------------
|      LEGGETT        |
|   MYRTLE   JESSE G  |
|  1887-1958 1876-1945 |
-----------------------


--------------------   -----------------
| JESSE H LEGGETT |   |  JACK KOONS   |
|    1914-1972    |   |  MAY 14 1918  |
--------------------   -----------------


-----------------------
|      REINKE         |
|  JULIUS    AUGUSTA  |
|  1848-1934 1849-1937 |
-----------------------


-----------------------
|      REINKE         |
|  WILLIAM F    EMILIA |
|  1884-1948   1887-19 |
-----------------------
```

Parkville Cemetery, Park Township, MI

Directions: From Interstate 94, exit at US131 (exit 74A) and travel south 15.5 miles to Moorepark Road. Turn east onto Moorepark and travel 4 miles to the cemetery entrance on the south side of the road.

112

```
--------------------------
|         SUSAN          |
|        wife of         |
|     Isaac Boudeman     |
|       and dau of       |
| Jno & Elizabeth Fortner |
|         Died           |
|       FEB 20 1871      |
|       at 64 Yrs        |
|         6 Ds           |
--------------------------
```

```
-------------   -------------
| WILLIAM   |   |  ISAAC    |
| BOUDEMAN  |   | BOUDEMAN  |
| 1837-1920 |   | 1804-1894 |
-------------   -------------
```

```
-------------   -------------
|  BELL     |   |  SARAH    |
| BOUDEMAN  |   | BOUDEMAN  |
| 1873-1908 |   | 1849-1936 |
-------------   -------------
```

Prairie River Cemetery, Centreville, MI

Directions: From Interstate 94, exit at US131 (exit 74A) and travel south 18 miles to Business 131/Main St. Turn onto Main and travel south 2 miles to M86. Continue on M86 6.5 miles to North Nottawa St. Turn north onto Nottawa and travel .4 miles to cemetery entrance on the east side of the road.

```
-------------------------------
|   MARY      |     MARY      |
|   KLOKO     |   Frau des    |
|             |  FRED KLOKO   |
|   Gest      |     Gest      |
| Mar 15 1855 | Julei 14 1883 |
|   Alter     |    Alter      |
| 65 Yar 8 Mon | 65 Yar 1 Mon |
|  24 Tagen   |   14 Tagen    |
-------------------------------
```

```
----------------         ---------------
| ELLA E HAZEL |         | GUY O HAZEL |
|  1889-1967   |         |  1885-1923  |
----------------         ---------------


----------------         ----------------
| HERMAN KLOKO |         | MINNIE KLOKO |
|  1860-1921   |         |  1861-1936   |
----------------         ----------------


          ----------------
          | EDWARD KLOKO |
          |  1885-1935   |
          ----------------


-------------------      -------------------
| EDITH M KRAMER  |      | HENRY P KRAMER  |
|    1888-1974    |      |    1881-1963    |
-------------------      -------------------


       ----------------------------
       |    LAWRENCE I KRAMER      |
       |     1st Lt  US Army       |
       |       World War II        |
       |  Feb 4 1913  Aug 27 1977  |
       ----------------------------


----------------         ----------------
|    Mother    |         |    Father    |
| HENRIETTA F  |         | CHRISTIAN C  |
|    KLOKO     |         |    KLOKO     |
|  1860-1951   |         |  1855-1939   |
----------------         ----------------


       ------------------------
       |         KLOKO        |
       |   ELLA L     HENRY W |
       | 1890-1974  1882-1968 |
       ------------------------


-----------------------------------
|              HAZEL              |
|  JAMES F   married  DOROTHEA E  |
|  1916-2002  July 2  1916-2009   |
|              1938               |
-----------------------------------
```

```
----------      --------------------
| -can-  |      | SOLOMON BOWERSOX |
| -not-  |      |       Co A        |
| -read- |      |     208 PA INF    |
----------      --------------------


        --------------------
        | ROBERT BOWERSOX |
        |    1871-1934     |
        --------------------


    -------------      -------------
    | MARTIN T  |      |  ALINE M  |
    | BOWERSOX  |      | BOWERSOX  |
    | 1870-1934 |      | 1875-1967 |
    -------------      -------------
```

Riverside Cemetery, Three Rivers, MI

Directions: From Interstate 94, exit at US131 (exit 74A) and travel south 18 miles to Business131/Main St. Turn south onto Bus131 and travel 2 miles to East Michigan St. Turn east onto Michigan and travel .5 miles to cemetery entrance on the east side of the road.

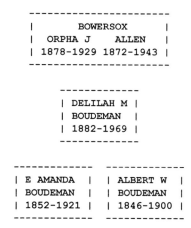

```
    ------------------------
    |         BOWERSOX      |
    |  ORPHA J    ALLEN     |
    | 1878-1929 1872-1943   |
    ------------------------


        -------------
        | DELILAH M |
        | BOUDEMAN  |
        | 1882-1969 |
        -------------


    -------------      -------------
    | E AMANDA  |      | ALBERT W  |
    | BOUDEMAN  |      | BOUDEMAN  |
    | 1852-1921 |      | 1846-1900 |
    -------------      -------------
```

Saint Joseph Cemetery, Watervliet, MI

Directions: From Interstate 94, exit at M-140 (exit 41) and travel north .5 miles to Red Arrow highway. Turn west onto Red Arrow and travel .6 miles to the cemetery entrance on the south side of the road.

```
           ----------
          |  DANIEL  |
           ----------

 -------------     -------------
| BRUNO Sr    |   | FRANCES M   |
| 1898 1972   |   | 1901 1973   |
 -------------     -------------

 -------------     -------------
| BRUNO Jr    |   |  JUNE M     |
| 1923 1951   |   | 1925 1996   |
 -------------     -------------
```

Saint Michaels Cemetery, Radom, IL

Directions: From Interstate 57, exit at IL-15 (exit 95) and travel west 13 miles to County Highway 23. Turn south onto CR-23 and travel 3 miles, turning west becoming Main Street. Continue traveling west on Main .5 miles to 3rd Street. Turn south onto 3rd and travel 1.0 miles to the cemetery entrance on the west side of the road.

```
 ----------------------------
|           DUDEK            |
|   EUGENE R     STELLA M    |
| July 23 1917  Apr 29 1918  |
| May  6 1987   Mar  9 1978  |
 ----------------------------

 --------------------------
|      EUGENE R DUDEK       |
|        Sgt US Army        |
|        World War II       |
| JUL 23 1917 MAY 6 1987    |
 --------------------------
```

```
-------------------------------
|           DUDEK             |
|  STANLEY J    CATHERINE M   |
|  Mar  23 1926  Oct 12 1925  |
|  June 16 1980               |
-------------------------------


----------------------------
|     STANLEY J DUDEK       |
|       Cpl US Army         |
|       World War II        |
|  MAR 23 1926 JUN 16 1980  |
----------------------------
```

Salem Cemetery, Alhambra, IL

Directions: From Interstate 55, exit at I-140 (exit 30) and travel east 6.0 miles to Alhambra Road. Turn north onto Alhambra and travel 1.1 miles to the cemetery entrance on the east side of the road.

```
 -------------   -------------
| HENSCHEN    | | HENSCHEN    |
| EDUARD H    | |  ALIDA      |
| 1884-1956   | | 1891-1974   |
 -------------   -------------


 ----------------------   ------------------
|     Mother           | |                  |
| DENNIE C HENSCHEN    | | ANNA E HOLMER    |
|   1893 - 1930        | |  1870 - 1944     |
 ----------------------   ------------------
```

Sherman Township Cemetery, Sherman Township, MI

Directions: From Interstate 94, exit at US131 (exit 74A) and travel south 18 miles to Business131/Main St. Turn south and travel 2 miles to M86. Continue south then east on M86 for 7.5 miles to Shimmel Road. Turn south on Shimmel and travel 3.5 miles to Banker St. Turn east onto Banker and travel .2 miles to cemetery entrance on the south side of the road.

117

```
-------------------------------------
|   FRIEDRICH    |    SOPHIA      |
|    BAUMAN      |    BAUMAN      |
|    Geboren     |     Geb        |
| Den 11 Mar 1816 | 23 Mai 1820   |
|    Gestorben   |     Gest       |
| Den 18 Sep 1882 | 17 Dez 1895   |
|    BAUMAN      |                |
-------------------------------------
```

```
-------------------------------
|     FRED      |    SOPHIA    |
|    BAUMAN     |    BAUMAN    |
| Jul 22 1849   | Aug  8 1853  |
| Dec 27 1898   | Apr 25 1903  |
|    BAUMAN     |              |
-------------------------------
```

```
-------------------
| ALBERT BAUMAN   |
|   Dec 14 1879   |
|   Oct 11 1946   |
-------------------
```

```
------------
| BAUMAN   |
------------
```

```
--------------    --------------
|   AUGUST    |   |   MINNIE    |
| 1854-1914   |   | 1860-1940   |
--------------    --------------
```

```
--------------    ----------------------
| LOUIS F   |   |     GERTRUDE         |
| 1889-1942 |   | Mar 8 1913 Sept 4    |
--------------    ----------------------
```

Silverbrook Cemetery, Niles, MI

Directions: From US31, turn onto Main Street and head east through downtown. Stay on Main Street, which turns right at a light, 1.0 miles to cemetery entrance on the south corner of East Main (business route 12) and Cherry Street.

```
---------------------------------
|           REED               |
|     Dad          Mom         |
|   WILLIAM      JOSEPHINE      |
|  Jan  2 1897   Oct  27 1906  |
|  Sept 22 1976  Nov  23 1998  |
---------------------------------

---------------------------------
|       WILLIAM REED Jr        |
|         Michigan             |
|          S1 USNR             |
|        World War II          |
|  OCT 28 1926 JULY 29 1951    |
---------------------------------

        -----------------
        | FREDERICK H |
        |    REED     |
        |  1928-1928  |
        -----------------

  -------------   -------------
  |  SARAH E  |   |  EZRA H   |
  |   REED    |   |   REED    |
  | 1866-1927 |   | 1860-1936 |
  -------------   -------------

        -----------------
        | MAY Dau  of |
        |  EH & SE    |
        |   REED      |
        |  1905-1918  |
        -----------------

      -----------------------
      |      LEGGETT        |
      | BERTHA M     FRED   |
      | 1874-1947 1871-1951 |
      |  MOTHER     FATHER  |
      -----------------------

-------------------------------------------
|               LEGGETT                   |
|  Father       Daughter       Mother     |
|  VICTOR J     BONNIE J       ANNA E     |
|  Jan 15 1909  Mar  1 1942  July 7 1915  |
|  Jan 23 1980  July 30 1986  May  9 1996 |
-------------------------------------------
```

119

```
-------------
|   MABLE   |
|  FRANCES  |
| 1916 1919 |
-------------
```

```
----------------------------
| ERVIN L   BERNICE KLOKO  |
|  KLOKO        SHISLEY    |
| 1899-1949    1902-1957   |
----------------------------
```

```
----------------------------
|     KENNETH C KLOKO      |
|        Michigan          |
|    Sgt 22 Bomb CP AAF    |
|      World War II        |
| DEC 20 1921   JUNE 3 1968 |
----------------------------
```

```
----------------------------
|          KLOKO           |
|  SHIRLEY E       DALE R  |
| Sept 26 1924  March 3 1923 |
|               July 3 2000 |
----------------------------
```

```
----------------
| MARY KLOKO   |
| NOV 10 1941  |
----------------
```

```
----------------------------
|     WALTER A HOLMER      |
|       TEC4 US Army       |
|       World War II       |
| DEC 12 1920   MAR 14 1975 |
----------------------------
```

State Hospital Cemetery, Kankakee, IL

Directions: From Interstate 57, exit at US45 (exit 308) and travel north 1.1 miles to River Road. Turn east onto River and travel 1.6 miles to South 1500 East Road. Turn north onto S1500e and travel .25 miles to the cemetery entrance on the west side of the road.

```
 --------
| 1289 |
 --------
```

Thornton Township Cemetery, Thornton, IL
   Directions: From Interstate 94, exit at Torrence Avenue
(exit 161) and travel south .6 miles to Thornton-Lansing
Road. Turn west onto Thornton-Lansing and travel 3.4 miles
to Ridge Road. Turn south onto Ridge and travel .3 miles to
the cemetery entrance on the north side of the road.

```
 ----------------   --------------------
|   ALLAN L     |  | WELDEN DuBREUIL |
|   DuBREUIL    |  | Beloved Husband |
| SEPT 29 1883  |  |   Of  Blanche   |
| JUNE  6 1917  |  |   1882 - 1937   |
 ----------------   --------------------


 ----------------   ----------------
|  MARTHA J     |  |  WILLIAM A   |
|  DuBREUIL     |  |  DuBREUIL    |
| MAY   9 1852  |  | JULY 4 1849  |
| JAN 16 1920   |  | NOV 14 1916  |
 ----------------   ----------------


     -----------------------------
    |    JOHN L     |              |
    |    Born       |              |
    | DEC 24 1852   |              |
    |    Died       |              |
    | SEP 21 1860   |              |
    |               |  AUGUSTUS    |
    |    JOHN       |  DuBREUIL    |
    |    Born       |              |
    | DEC 22 1861   |    Born      |
    |    Died       | MAR  9 1821  |
    | NOV 18 1864   |    Died      |
    |               | JUL 20 1875  |
    |   HATTIE E    |              |
    |    Born       |              |
    | DEC 22 1865   |              |
    |    Died       |              |
    | MAR  1 1868   |              |
     -----------------------------
```

121

```
--------------------   --------------------
| LOA E DuBREUIL |  | FOREST DuBREUIL |
|  July 20 1875 |  |  MAR 26 1888    |
|  Sept 24 1885 |  |  NOV 22 1945    |
--------------------   --------------------
```

```
--------------------
|   RUSSELL H      |
|    DuBREUIL      |
|   1892-1923      |
|   Erected By     |
| MATTIE D BARNARD |
--------------------
```

Watervliet Cemetery, Watervliet, MI

Directions: From Interstate 94, exit at M-140 (exit 41) and travel north .5 miles to Red Arrow highway. Turn east onto Red Arrow and travel .2 miles to the cemetery entrance on the north side of the road.

```
---------------
|   Mother    |
| HELEN BECHT |
| 1897   1968 |
---------------
```

Appendix D:
Who's Who

Barczak, Dolores (1926-1995) Dolores was born Dolores Hermanski in 1926 in Chicago, Illinois. She grew up in South Chicago, being the youngest of two siblings. She married Tim Barczak. They had children. She passed away in February of 1995. She was about 68 years old. She was buried on February 18, 1995 at Holy Cross Cemetery in Calumet City, Illinois.

Bauman, Albert A (1879-1946) Albert was born on December 14, 1879. He grew up in Michigan, being the fourth child of eight siblings. Albert passed away on October 11, 1946. He was 66 years old. He was buried at Sherman Township Cemetery in Sherman, Michigan.

Bauman, Augustus Frederick Carl (1854-1914) Augustus was born on May 23, 1854 in Germany. He grew up being the middle child of three siblings. He immigrated to the United States with his family in 1861. Augustus married Minnie. They had four children. He was a farmer. Augustus passed away from Paralysis on February 12, 1914 in Sherman, Michigan. He was 59 years old. He was buried on February 15, 1914 at Sherman Township Cemetery in Sherman, Michigan.

Bauman, Frederick (1816-1882) Frederick was born on March 11, 1816 in Germany. He married Sophia Stry. They had three children. He immigrated with his family to the United States in 1861. He was a farmer. Frederick passed away from Apoplexy on September 18, 1882 in Sherman, Michigan. He was 66 years old. He was buried at Sherman Township Cemetery in Sherman, Michigan.

Bauman, Frederick (1849-1898) Frederick was born on July 22, 1849 in Germany. He grew up being the eldest of three siblings. He immigrated to the United States with his family in 1861. Frederick was married in 1871 to Sophia. They had eight children. He was a farmer. Frederick passed away from Apoplexy on December 27, 1898 in Sherman, Michigan. He was 49 years old. He was buried on December 30, 1898 at Sherman Township Cemetery in Sherman, Michigan.

Bauman, Sophia (1820-1895) Sophia was born Sophia Stry on May 23, 1820 in Germany. She married Frederick Bauman. They had three children. She immigrated with her family to the United States in 1861. Sophia passed away on December 17, 1895. She was 75 years old. She was buried at Sherman Township Cemetery in Sherman, Michigan.

Becht, Helen Irene (1897-1968) Helen was born Helen Szczesniak on May 9, 1897 in Chicago, Illinois. She grew up in South Chicago, being the third child of seven siblings. Helen was married to Austin Walter Holmer. They had three children. They were divorced on May 23, 1935. She remarried on September 22, 1935 to Joseph J Sadowski at St Mary's Church in Paw Paw, Michigan. They had no children.

She became widowed on June 11, 1937. She was also remarried to Edson Becht, having no children. Helen passed away from Ventricular Fibulation due to Arteriosclerotic Heart Disease, Hypertension and Diabetes Mellitus on October 21, 1968 in Coloma, Michigan. She was 71 years old. She was buried on October 24, 1968 at Watervliet Cemetery in Watervliet, Michigan.

Boudeman, Albert (1846-1900) Albert was born in 1846. He grew up in Michigan, being the youngest of six siblings. Albert married Amanda Seas. They had two children. Albert passed away in 1900. He was about 54 years old. He was buried at Riverside Cemetery in Three Rivers, Michigan.

Boudeman, E Amanda (1852-1921) Amanda was born Amanda Seas on July 13, 1852 in Pennsylvania. She grew up in Michigan, being the youngest of five siblings. Amanda married Albert Boudeman. They had two children. Amanda passed away on June 14, 1921. She was 68 years old. She was buried at Riverside Cemetery in Three Rivers, Michigan.

Boudeman, Isaac (1804-1894) Isaac was born in 1804. He married Susan Fortner. They had six children. Isaac passed away in 1894. He was about 90 years old. He was buried at Parkville Cemetery in Parkville, Michigan.

Boudeman, Susan (1807-1871) Susan was born Susan Fortner on February 14, 1807 in New Jersey. She married Isaac Boudeman. They had six children. Susan passed away from Abscesis Bowels on February 20, 1871 in Park, Michigan. She was 64 years old. She was buried at Parkville Cemetery in Parkville, Michigan.

Bowersox, Allen (1872-1943) Allen was born on September 19, 1872. He grew up in Michigan, being the fourth child of ten siblings. Allen was married on May 13, 1899 to Orpha Jane Boudeman. They had six children. He was also a farmer. Allen passed away from Acute Cardiac Failure on January 12, 1943 in Three Rivers, Michigan. He was 70 years old. He was buried on January 15, 1943 at Riverside Cemetery in Three Rivers, Michigan.

Bowersox, Lydia Elizabeth (1843-1880) Lydia was born Lydia Kerr on July 11, 1843 in Pennsylvania. She was married on January 19, 1868 to Solomon Bowersox. They had six children. Lydia passed away on September 9, 1880 in Three Rivers, Michigan. She was 37 years old. She was buried at Prairie River Cemetery in Centreville, Michigan.

Bowersox, Orpha Jane (1878-1929) Orpha was born Orpha Boudeman on March 7, 1878. She grew up in Michigan, being the youngest of two siblings. Orpha was married on May 13, 1899 to Allen Bowersox. They had six children. Orpha passed away from Carcinoma of Rectum on January 2, 1929 in Three Rivers, Michigan. She was 50 years old. She was buried at Riverside Cemetery in Three Rivers, Michigan.

Bowersox, Solomon J (1845-1918) Solomon was born on March 25, 1845 in Pennsylvania. He was married on January 19, 1868 to Lydia Kerr. They had six children. He became widowed on September 9, 1880. He remarried Dora. They had four children. He was a laborer on a farm. Solomon passed away from General Paratis on July 2, 1918 in Three Rivers, Michigan. He was 73 years old. He was buried at Prairie River Cemetery in Centreville, Michigan.

Briggs, George Lanson (1879-1907) George was born on June 11, 1879 in Elk Rapids, Michigan. He was the youngest of eight siblings. He was married. He was a stone mason. George passed away from Diabetes Mellitis on September 8, 1907 in East Bay, Michigan. He was 28 years old. He was buried on September 10, 1907 at Oak Wood Cemetery in Traverse City, Michigan.

Briggs, Harry James (1865-1917) Harry was born on September 13, 1865 in Coaticook, Quebec, Canada. He grew up in Michigan, being the fourth child of eight siblings. Harry was married on October 26, 1885 to Nellie E McCauley in Beaver Island, Michigan. They had ten children. He was a publisher. Harry passed away from Acute Ulceration Endocarditis due to Influenza on November 24, 1917 in Elk Rapids, Michigan. He was 52 years old. He was buried on November 27, 1917 in Kewadin, Michigan.

Briggs, Harry James (1888-1917) Harry was born on December 26, 1888. He grew up in Michigan, being the second child of ten siblings. Harry never married. He was a chemist. Harry passed away from Hemorrhage due to Pulmonary Tuberculosis on July 5, 1917 in Elk Rapids, Michigan. He was 28 years old. He was buried on July 7, 1917 in Kewadin, Michigan.

Briggs, James J (1831-1911) James was born on August 25, 1831 in Swansea, Wales. He married Eliza Barber in Canada. They had eight children. He was a mason. James passed away from Chronic Endocarditis on April 27, 1911 in Elk Rapids, Michigan. He was 79 years old. He was buried on April 28, 1911 in Elk Rapids, Michigan.

Clark, Joan Gwyndolyn (1931-2003) Joan was born Joan Huskey on October 25, 1931 in Kalamazoo, Michigan. She grew up in Michigan, being the second child of six living siblings. Joan was married on November 17, 1951 to Kenneth E Clark. They had five children. Joan passed away on November 1, 2003 in Kalamazoo, Michigan. She was 72 years old. She was buried on November 5, 2003 at North Shore Memory Gardens in Hagar Shores, Michigan.

Clark, Kenneth E (1952-1994) Kenny was born on June 12, 1952 in Benton Harbor, Michigan. He grew up in Coloma, being the eldest of five siblings. Kenny married and had children. Kenny passed away on July 17, 1994 in St. Joseph, Michigan. He was 42 years old. He was buried on July 21, 1994 at North Shore Memory Gardens in Hagar Shores, Michigan.

Clark, LaDonna Lynn (1967-1984) LaDonna was born on March 1, 1967 in Benton Harbor, Michigan. She grew up in Coloma, being the youngest of five siblings. She never married. LaDonna passed away on August 19, 1984 in St. Joseph, Michigan. She was 17 years old. She was buried on August 22, 1984 at North Shore Memory Gardens in Hagar Shores, Michigan.

Cross, Abner (1828-1894) Abner was born in 1828. He was born the third child of six siblings. He married and had two children. He served in the Michigan Cavalry. Abner passed away in 1894. He was about 66 years old. He was buried at Lakeview Cemetery in South Haven, Michigan.

Cross, Albert (1826-1902) Albert was born in 1826 in New York. He was born the second child of six siblings.

He married Jane Herson. They had four children. He was a farmer. Albert passed away in 1902. He was about 76 years old. He was buried at Lakeview Cemetery in South Haven, Michigan.

Cross, Albert J (1889-1978) Albert was born in 1889 in South Haven, Michigan. He was born the third child of four siblings. Albert passed away in August of 1978. He was about 89 years old. He was buried at Lakeview Cemetery in South Haven, Michigan.

Cross, Alonzo Barney (1853-1914) Alonzo was born in 1853. He grew up in Michigan, being the eldest of four siblings. He married Harriet MacDonald. They had four children. Alonzo passed away in 1914. He was about 51 years old.

Cross, Caroline (1810-1915) Caroline was born Caroline Pauling on April 5, 1810 in Germany. She married Wesley Cross. They had six children. Caroline passed away from Senile Debility on February 1, 1915 in Coloma, Michigan. She was 104 years old. She was buried at Coloma Cemetery in Coloma, Michigan.

Cross, Ceylon M (1856-1922) Ceylon was born around 1856. He grew up in Michigan, being the fifth child of six siblings. Ceylon married Magdaline. They had six children. Ceylon passed away in 1922. He was about 66 years old. He was buried at Lakeview Cemetery in South Haven, Michigan.

Cross, Charlotte (1860-?) Charlotte was born Charlotte Briggs in 1860 in Canada. She was second child of eight siblings. Charlotte was married on December 8, 1878 to Eugene Cross in Traverse City, Michigan. They had five children.

Cross, Eugene (1854-?) Eugene was born in 1854 in Galesburg, Michigan. He grew up in South Haven, being the fourth child of six siblings. Eugene was married on December 8, 1878 to Charlotte Briggs in Traverse City, Michigan. They had five children.

Cross, Mary (1887-1888) Mary was born on May 24, 1887 in South Haven, Michigan. She was born the first child of four siblings. Mary passed away on October 3, 1888. She was 16 months and 9 days old. She was buried at Lakeview Cemetery in South Haven, Michigan.

Cross, Nelson A (1857-1883) Nelson was born in 1857. He grew up in Michigan, being the second child of four siblings. Nelson passed away in 1883. He was about 26 years old. He was buried at Lakeview Cemetery in South Haven, Michigan.

Cross, Polly (1793-?) Polly was born Polly Jones around 1793. She married Enoch Cross. They had six children.

Cross, Roy (1880-1892) Roy was born about 1880. He grew up in Michigan, being the second child of five siblings. Roy passed away from Inflammation of Stomach on January 24, 1892 in Charlevoix, Michigan. He was 12 years old. He was buried in Charlevoix Cemetery in Charlevoix, Michigan.

Cross, Viola (1903-1904) Viola was born on May 30, 1903 in Illinois. She was born the youngest of seven siblings.

Viola passed away from Heart Failure due to Colitis on June 28, 1904 in Charlevoix, Michigan. She was 12 months and 28 days old. She was buried on June 29, 1904 at Charlevoix Cemetery in Charlevoix, Michigan.

Cross, Wesley (1809-1899) Wesley was born on February 25, 1809 in New York. He was born the eldest of six siblings. He was married in 1832 to Caroline Pauling. They had seven children. He was a sailor. Wesley passed away from Filling with Mucus in Lungs due to Senile Debility due to Old Age on November 1, 1899 in Charlevoix, Michigan. He was 90 years old. He was buried on November 2, 1899 at Charlevoix Cemetery in Charlevoix, Michigan.

Daniel, Bruno Francis (1923-1961) Bruno was born Bruno Jasinski Jr on December 1, 1923 in Chicago, Illinois. He grew up in Michigan, being an only child. He married June. They had one child. Bruno passed away on November 10, 1961. He was 37 years old. He was buried on November 14, 1961 at St Joseph Cemetery in Watervliet, Michigan.

Daniel, Frances M (1901-1973) Frances was born Frances Szczesniak on December 1, 1901 in Chicago, Illinois. She grew up in South Chicago, being the fifth child of seven siblings. Frances married Bruno Jasinski. They had one child. Frances passed away in January of 1973. She was 71 years old. She was buried at St Joseph Cemetery in Watervliet, Michigan.

DePue, Edna E (1894-1966) Edna was born Edna Kloko on March 15, 1894. She grew up in Michigan, being the fourth child of five siblings. Edna married LaVern DePue. They had two children. Edna passed away on January 21, 1966 in Three Rivers, Michigan. She was 71 years old. She was buried on January 24, 1966 at Mendon Cemetery in Mendon, Michigan.

DuBreuil, Allan L (1883-1917) Allan was born on September 29, 1883 in Chicago, Illinois. He grew up in Illinois, being the middle child of seven siblings. Allan married Myrtle Alice Cross. They had one child. Allan passed away on June 6, 1917. He was 33 years old. He was buried at Thornton Township Cemetery in Thornton, Illinois.

DuBreuil, Augustus (1821-1875) Augustus was born on March 9, 1821 in Canada. He married Elizabeth. They had five children. Augustus passed away on July 20, 1875. He was 54 years old. He was buried at Thornton Township Cemetery in Thornton, Illinois.

DuBreuil, Edward A (1869-?) Edward was born around 1869 in Indiana. He was born the youngest of five siblings. He married Anna Garceau in Canada. They had children.

DuBreuil, Elizabeth A (1832-1892) Elizabeth was born about 1832. She married Augustus DuBreuil. They had five children. She became widowed on July 20, 1875. She was remarried on August 5, 1876 to John L DuBreuil at the Palmer residence in Chicago, Illinois. They had no children. Elizabeth passed away from Cerebral Apoplexy on September 17, 1892 in Chicago, Illinois. She was about 60 years old. She was buried at Thornton Township Cemetery in Thornton, Illinois.

DuBreuil, Forest F (1888-1945) Forest was born on March 26, 1888. He grew up in Illinois, being the fifth child of seven siblings. Forest passed away on November 22, 1945. He was 57 years old. He was buried at Thornton Township Cemetery in Thornton, Illinois.

DuBreuil, Hattie E (1865-1868) Hattie was born on December 22, 1865. She was born the fourth child of five siblings. Hattie passed away on March 1, 1868. She was 2 years old. She was buried at Thornton Township Cemetery in Thornton, Illinois.

DuBreuil, John (1861-1864) John was born on December 22, 1861. He was born the middle child of five siblings. John passed away on November 18, 1864. He was 2 years old. He was buried at Thornton Township Cemetery in Thornton, Illinois.

DuBreuil, John L (1823-1891) John was born in 1823 in Canada. He was married on August 5, 1876 to Elizabeth A DuBreuil at the Palmer residence in Chicago, Illinois. They had no children. John passed away from La Grippe on April 18, 1891 in Chicago, Illinois. He was 68 years old. He was buried at Thornton Township Cemetery in Thornton, Illinois.

DuBreuil, John L (1852-1860) John L was born on December 24, 1852 in New York. He was born the second child of five siblings. John L passed away on September 21, 1860. He was 7 years old. He was buried at Thornton Township Cemetery in Tornton, Illinois.

DuBreuil, Loa E (1875-1885) Loa was born on July 20, 1875 in Illinois. She was the eldest of seven siblings. She never married. Loa passed away on September 24, 1885. She was 10 years old. She was buried at Thornton Township Cemetery in Thornton, Illinois.

DuBreuil, Mattie J (1852-1920) Mattie was born Martha Holbrook on May 9, 1852 in Illinois. She grew up in Illinois, being the youngest of four siblings. She was married on September 17, 1874 to William A DuBreuil in Cook County, Illinois. They had seven children. Mattie passed away from Chronic Interstitial Nephritis due to Acute Attack of Colic Cystitis on January 16, 1920 at her residence in Chicago, Illinois. She was 67 years old. She was buried on January 19, 1920 at Thornton Township Cemetery in Thornton, Illinois.

DuBreuil, Russell H (1892-1923) Russell was born on October 19, 1892 in Canada. He married Florence. He was a Delicatessen owner. Russell passed away from Diabetes Mellitus on September 3, 1923 in Chicago, Illinois. He was 30 years old. He was buried on September 5, 1923 at Thornton Township Cemetery in Thornton, Illinois.

DuBreuil, Welden B (1882-1937) Welden was born in 1882. He grew up in Illinois, being the third child of seven siblings. He married Blanche. Welden passed away in 1937. He was about 55 years old. He was buried in Thornton Township Cemetery in Thornton, Illinois.

DuBreuil, William A (1849-1916) William was born on July 4, 1849 in New York. He was the eldest of five siblings. William was married on September 17, 1874 to Martha

J Holbrook in Cook County, Illinois. They had seven children. William passed away from Chronic Myocarditis on November 14, 1916 in Englewood, Illinois. He was 67 years old. He was buried on November 17, 1916 at Thornton Township Cemetery in Thornton, Illinois.

DuBreuil, Winfield R (1891-1923) Winfield was born about 1891. He grew up in Illinois, being the sixth child of seven siblings. He married Mary. They had children. Winfield passed away on September 3, 1923. He was about 32 years old.

Dudek, Eugene R (1917-1987) Eugene was born on July 23, 1917 in Chicago, Illinois. He grew up in South Chicago, being the eldest of his siblings. He married Stella. They had children. He became widowed on March 9, 1978. He remarried, having no children. He served in the U.S. Army during World War II. Eugene passed away on May 6, 1987. He was 69 years old. He was buried at St Michael's Cemetery in Radom, Illinois.

Dudek, Mary (1895-1980) Mary was born Mary Szczesniak on March 25, 1895 in Chicago, Illinois. She grew up in South Chicago, being the second child of seven siblings. Mary was married on November 24, 1915 to Stanley Dudek in Chicago, Illinois. They had children. Mary passed away on January 10, 1980. She was 84 years old.

Dudek, Stanley J (1926-1980) Stanley was born on March 23, 1926 in Chicago, Illinois. He grew up in South Chicago. He married Catherine. They had children. He served in the U.S. Army during World War II. Stanley passed away on

June 16, 1980. He was 54 years old. He was buried at St Michael's Cemetery in Radom, Illinois.

Hazel, Ella Edith (1889-1967) Ella was born Ella Kloko on August 1, 1889. She grew up in Michigan, being the middle child of five siblings. She married Guy Hazel. They had one child. Ella passed away on October 8, 1967. She was 78 years old. She was buried on October 11, 1967 at Prairie River Cemetery in Centreville, Michigan.

Hazel, James F (1916-2002) James was born on October 12, 1916. He grew up in Michigan, being an only child. He was married on July 2, 1938 to Dorothea. They had two children. James passed away in 2002. He was about 86 years old. He was buried at Prairie River Cemetery in Centreville, Michigan.

Henschen, Alida (1891-1974) Alida was born Alida Holmer on April 30, 1891 in Chicago, Illinois. She grew up in South Chicago, being the middle of three siblings. Alida was married to Eduard H Henschen, having no children. Alida passed away from Cardiac Arrest due to Arteriosclerotic Heart Disease on January 26, 1974 in Pocahontas, Illinois. She was 82 years old. She was buried on January 30, 1974 at Salem Cemetery in Alhambra, Illinois.

Hermanski, Wladyshaw (1904-1971) Lottie was born Wladyshaw Szczesniak in 1904 in Chicago, Illinois. She grew up in South Chicago, being the sixth child of seven siblings. Lottie married Sylvester Hermanski. They had two children. Lottie passed away in June of 1971. She was about 67 years old. She was buried on June 12, 1971 at Holy Cross

Cemetery in Calumet City, Illinois.

Holbrook, Clark (1838-1904) Clark was born in 1838. He grew up in Illinois, being the eldest of four siblings. Clark was married on May 7, 1863 to Anne Raymond. They had five children. Clark passed away on February 21, 1904. He was about 65 years old. He was buried at Fremont Holbrook Cemetery in Homewood, Illinois.

Holbrook, Fremont (1850-1926) Fremont was born in 1850. He grew up in Illinois, being the third child of four siblings. Fremont was married on October 10, 1877 to Phoebe Ann Brown. They had three children. Fremont passed away on July 26, 1926. He was about 76 years old. He was buried at Fremont Holbrook Cemetery in Homewood, Illinois.

Holbrook, Joseph R (1814-1881) Joseph was born in 1814. He married Mary. They had four children. Joseph passed away in 1881. He was about 67 years old. He was buried at Fremont Holbrook Cemetery in Homewood, Illinois.

Holbrook, Mary E (1817-1884) Mary was born in 1817. She married Joseph R Holbrook. They had four children. Mary passed away in 1884. She was about 67 years old. She was buried at Fremont Holbrook Cemetery in Homewood, Illinois.

Holbrook, Nahum (1840-?) Nahum was born about 1840. He grew up in Illinois, being the second child of four siblings. Nahum married Clarissa Sue. They had five children.

Holmer, Albert Walter (1919-2009) Albert was born on March 25, 1919 in Chicago, Illinois. He grew up in South Chicago, being the middle of three brothers. Albert was married on December 26, 1939 to Rhama Huskey in Crown Point, Indiana. They had three children. He became widowed on August 12, 1976. He remarried on November 20, 1976 to Mary Lillian Holmer at the Coloma Bible Church in Coloma, Michigan. They had no children. Albert was a security guard for corporate security. He also served in the U.S. Navy during World War II, 1944-1945. Albert passed away from Urosepsis due to Dehydration due to Dementia on December 7, 2009 in Coloma, Michigan. He was 90 years old. He was cremated, and his ashes were buried on June 18, 2010 at Coloma Cemetery in Coloma, Michigan.

Holmer, Anna Emilia (1870-1944) Anna was born Anna Anderson on June 4, 1870 in Gattenberg, Sweden. She was married on October 27, 1888 to John Holmer at the Svenka Ev. Lutherska Elim Church in Pullman, Illinois. They had three children. Anna passed away from Carcinoma of Breast on June 10, 1944 in Leif, Illinois. She was 74 years old. She was buried on June 11, 1944 at Salem Cemetery in Alhambra, Illinois.

Holmer, Arthur Joseph (1917-1969) Arthur was born on May 22, 1917 in Chicago, Illinois. He grew up in South Chicago, being the eldest of three brothers. Arthur was married and divorced, having no children. He was remarried on October 15, 1949 to Mary Lillian Lewis at the First Congregational Church in Benton Harbor, Michigan. They had two children. He was an assembler for a factory. Arthur passed away from Cardiac Arrhythmia due to Obstruction

Left and R Coronary Arteries on March 3, 1969 in Benton Harbor, Michigan. He was 51 years old. He was buried on March 6, 1969 at North Shore Memory Gardens in Hagar Shores, Michigan.

Holmer, Arthur V (1889-1955) Arthur was born in 1889 in Chicago, Illinois. He grew up in South Chicago, being the eldest of three siblings. Arthur was married to Ella Smith. They had one child. Arthur passed away in 1955. He was 66 years old. He was buried on March 30, 1955 at Cedar Park Cemetery in Calumet Park, Illinois.

Holmer, Austin Walter (1893-1967) Austin was born on July 18, 1893 in Chicago, Illinois. He grew up in South Chicago, being the youngest of three siblings. Austin was married to Helen Irene Szczesniak. They had three children. They were divorced on May 23, 1935. He remarried on June 29, 1935 to Helen Elizabeth Fogler in Gary, Indiana. They had no children. He was a carpenter. Austin passed away from Carcinoma of Lung on October 5, 1967 in Gary, Indiana. He was 74 years old. He was buried on October 7, 1967 at Calumet Park Cemetery in Gary, Indiana.

Holmer, Evangeline J (1916-1972) Evangeline was born in 1916 in Chicago, Illinois. She grew up in South Chicago, being an only child. She never married. Evangeline passed away in 1972. She was 56 years old. She was buried on November 4, 1972 at Cedar Park Cemetery in Calumet Park, Illinois.

Holmer, John Elbert (1863-1933) John was born on January 21, 1863 in Shono, Sweden. He was married on

October 27, 1888 to Anna Emilia Anderson at the Svenska Ev. Lutherska Elim Church in Pullman, Illinois. They had three children. He was a laborer for the Pullman factory. John passed away from Chronic Myocarditis on January 11, 1933 in Kankakee, Illinois. He was 69 years old. He was buried on January 19, 1933 at Kankakee State Hospital Cemetery #1289 in Kankakee, Illinois.

Holmer, Rhama Alene (1910-1976) Rhama was born Rhama DuBreuil on January 1, 1910 in Chicago, Illinois. She grew up in Michigan, being an only child. Rhama married Eber Warren Huskey. They had four children. They were divorced. She remarried Albert Holmer on December 26, 1939 in Crown Point, Indiana. They had three children. She was a waitress. Rhama passed away from Carcinoma of the Lung on August 12, 1976 in Berrien Center, Michigan. She was 66 years old. She was buried on August 16, 1976 at Coloma Cemetery in Coloma, Michigan.

Holmer, Walter Austin (1920-1975) Walter was born Lawrence Holmer on December 12, 1920 in Chicago, Illinois. He grew up in South Chicago, being the youngest of three brothers. Walter was married and divorced. He remarried on September 17, 1955 to Lillian Harriet Beck at the Plymouth Congregational Church in Watervliet, Michigan. They had one child. Walter was an electrician. He also served in the U.S. Army during World War II, 1942-1945. Walter passed away from Acute Ventricular Arrhythmia due to Coronary Artery Disease on March 14, 1975 in Niles, Michigan. He was 54 years old. He was buried on March 18, 1975 at Silverbrook Cemetery in Niles, Michigan.

Huskey, Eugene Warren (1929-1982) Eugene was born on October 24, 1929 in Kalamazoo, Michigan. He grew up in Michigan, being the eldest of six living siblings. Eugene was married on August 21, 1950 to Frances Enos in Michigan. They had three children. Eugene was an accountant. He also served in the U.S. Air Force. Eugene passed away on March 3, 1982 in Rapid City, South Dakota. He was 52 years old. He was buried March 6, 1982 at Mountain View Cemetery in Rapid City, South Dakota.

Huskey, Myrtle Alice (1935-1935) Myrtle Alice was born on April 15, 1935 in DeLand, Florida. She was born the middle child of seven. Myrtle Alice passed away on September 26, 1935 in De Land, Florida. She was five months and eleven days old. She was buried at the Clinton Family Cemetery by the Ariel Memorial Park in Oak Hill, Florida.

Kloko, Christian C (1855-1939) Christ was born in 1855 in Germany. He immigrated to the United States with his family in 1856. He was also adopted by Frederick Kloko. He grew up in Michigan, being the eldest of two siblings. Christ married Henrietta. They had four children. He was a farmer. Christ passed away in 1939. He was about 84 years old. He was buried at Prairie River Cemetery in Centreville, Michigan.

Kloko, Dale Richard (1923-2000) Dale was born on March 3, 1923. He grew up in Michigan, being the second child of six siblings. Dale married Shirley Dreibelbis at First Methodist Church in South bend, Indiana. They had four children. He served in the U.S. Army during World War II. Dale passed away on July 3, 2000. He was 77 years old. He was buried at Silverbrook Cemetery in Niles, Michigan.

Kloko, Edward F (1885-1935) Edward was born on April 18, 1885. He grew up in Michigan, being the eldest of five siblings. He never married. Edward passed away in 1935. He was about 50 years old. He was buried at Prairie River Cemetery in Centreville, Michigan.

Kloko, Ervin Louis (1899-1949) Ervin was born on April 4, 1899 in Nottawa, Michigan. He grew up the youngest of five siblings. Ervin married Bernice Bowersox. They had seven children. He worked on the railroad as Section foreman for New York Central. Ervin passed away from Coronary Occlusion on April 3, 1949 in Niles, Michigan. He was 49 years old. He was buried on April 6, 1949 at Silverbrook Cemetery in Niles, Michigan.

Kloko, Frederick (1833-1899) Frederick was born on May 26, 1833 in Schwichtenberg, Pomerania, Germany. He was the youngest of four siblings. He immigrated to the United States with his family in 1856. Frederick was married in 1857 to Mary Kloko. He adopted one child, and they had one child. He became widowed on July 14, 1883. He was remarried on June 19, 1887 to Friederike Bork in Michigan. They had no children. He was a farmer. Frederick passed away from Fatty Degeneration of Liver and Dropsey on January 4, 1899 in Sherman, Michigan. He was 65 years old. He was buried at the Old Church Cemetery.

Kloko, Henry W (1882-1968) Henry was born in 1882.

He grew up in Michigan, being the eldest of four children. Henry married Ella. They had children. Henry passed away in 1968. He was about 86 years old. He was buried at Prairie River Cemetery in Centreville, Michigan.

Kloko, Herman Frederick (1860-1921) Herman was born on April 14, 1860 in Buffalo, New York. He grew up in Michigan being the youngest of two siblings. Herman married Wihelmina Bauman. They had five children. He was a farmer. Herman passed away from Carcinoma of Throat on September 18, 1921 in Centreville, Michigan. He was 61 years old. He was buried at Prairie River Cemetery in Centreville, Michigan.

Kloko, Kenneth Carroll (1921-1968) Ken was born on December 20, 1921. He grew up in Michigan, being the eldest of six siblings. Ken married Virginia Hendershot. He served in the U.S. Air Force during World War II. Ken passed away on June 3, 1968. He was 46 years old. He was buried on June 6, 1968 at Silverbrook Cemetery in Niles, Michigan.

Kloko, Maria (1789-1855) Maria was born Maria Hall on June 19, 1789 in Germany. Maria married Christopher Kloko. They had four children. Maria passed away on March 15, 1855.

Kloko, Mary (1818-1883) Mary was born Mary Kuss on May 30, 1818 in Germany. Mary married George Kloko. They had one child. She became widowed. She was remarried in 1857 to Frederick Kloko. They had one child. Mary passed away from Spinal Complaint on July 14, 1883 in Sherman, Michigan. She was 65 years old. She was buried in the Old Church Cemetery. She was later moved to Prairie River Cemetery in Centreville, Michigan.

Kloko, Mary (1941) Mary Kloko was stillborn on November 10, 1941. She was buried on November 10, 1941 at Silverbrook Cemetery in Niles, Michigan.

Kloko, Paul Keith (1935-2005) Paul was born on August 31, 1935. He grew up in Michigan, being the youngest of six siblings. Paul married Emelyne Lane. They had four children. Paul passed away on January 20, 2005. He was 69 years old.

Kloko, Wilhelmina Fredericka Caroline (1861-1936) Minnie was born Wilhelmina Bauman on October 25, 1861 in Germany. She immigrated to the United States with her family in 1861. She grew up in Michigan, being the youngest of three siblings. Minnie married Herman Kloko. They had five children. Minnie passed away from Arterio Sclerosis on February 9, 1936. She was 74 years old. She was buried at Prairie River Cemetery in Centreville, Michigan.

Kramer, Edith M (1888-1974) Edith was born Edith Kloko on June 29, 1988. She grew up in Michigan, being the second child of five siblings. Edith married Henry Kramer. They had three children. Edith passed away in 1974. She was about 86 years old. She was buried at Prairie River Cemetery in Centreville, Michigan.

Kramer, Lawrence I (1913-1977) Lawrence was born on February 4, 1913. He grew up in Michigan, being the middle child of three siblings. He served in the U.S. Army during

World War II. Larence passed away on August 27, 1977. He was 64 years old. He was buried at Prairie River Cemetery in Centreville, Michigan.

Lancaster, Steven Craig (1951-1978) Steve was born on September 16, 1951 in Sturgis, Michigan. He grew up as the second child of six siblings. He never married. Steve passed away on October 20, 1978 in South Bend, Indiana. He was 27 years old. He was buried on October 23, 1978 in Burr Oak Township Cemetery in Burr Oak, Michigan.

Lazear, Alberta (1879-1927) Alberta was born Alberta Cross around 1879. She grew up in Michigan, the eldest of five siblings. She married Lincoln Lazear. They had no children. Alberta passed away on December 24, 1927. She was about 48 years old.

Leggett, Bertha M (1874-1947) Bertha was born Bertha Reinke on December 8, 1874 in Germany. She was the second child of five siblings. Bertha was married on February 9, 1897 to George Cauffman in Dayton, Michigan. They had three children. She became widowed. She was remarried on October 4, 1903 to Fred Leggett in Buchanan, Michigan. They had six children. Bertha passed away from Cerebral Hemorrhage due to Chronic Nephritis and Myocarditis on November 23, 1947 in Niles, Michigan. She was 72 years old. She was buried on November 26, 1947 at Silverbrook Cemetery in Niles, Michigan.

Leggett, Bonnie J (1942-1986) Bonnie was born on March 1, 1942. She grew up in Michigan. Bonnie passed away on July 30, 1986. She was 44 years old. She was buried at

Silverbrook Cemetery in Niles, Michigan.

Leggett, Esther L (1834-1910) Esther was born Esther Barnes on November 4, 1834 in New York. She married Jesse G Leggett. They had six children. Esther passed away from Abdominal Tumor on June 12, 1910 in Buchanan, Michigan. She was 75 years old. She was buried on June 14, 1910 at Oak Ridge Cemetery in Buchanan, Michigan.

Leggett, Fred (1871-1951) Fred was born on February 22, 1871. He grew up in Michigan, being the fifth child of six siblings. Fred was married on October 4, 1903 to Bertha Reinke in Buchanan, Michigan. They had six children. Fred was a painter. He also worked on the railroad as a mechanic. Fred passed away from Exsanguinating Hemorrhage and Shock due to Leukoplakia and Varices Esophagus due to Portal Cirrhosis on April 25, 1951 in Niles, Michigan. He was 80 years old. He was buried on April 27, 1951 at Silverbrook Cemetery in Niles, Michigan.

Leggett, Jesse G (1836-1892) Jesse was born in 1836. He married Esther Barnes. They had six children. Jesse passed away in 1892. He was about 56 years old. He was buried at Oak Ridge Cemetery in Buchanan, Michigan.

Leggett, Jesse G (1876-1945) Jesse was born in 1876. He grew up in Michigan, being the youngest child of six siblings. Jesse was married on June 16, 1911 to Daisy Myrtle Koons. Jesse passed away on October 2, 1876. He was about 69 years old. He was buried at Oak Ridge Cemetery in Buchanan, Michigan.

Leggett, Mable Frances (1916-1919) Mabel was born on November 21, 1916 in Niles, Michigan. She was the youngest of six siblings. Mabel passed away from Broncho Pneumonia due to Measles on March 12, 1919 in Niles, Michigan. She was 2 years old. She was buried on March 15, 1919 at Silverbrook Cemetery in Niles, Michigan.

Leggett, Victor John (1909-1980) Victor was born on January 15, 1909. He grew up in Michigan, being the third child of six siblings. He married and had children. Victor passed away on January 23, 1980. He was 71 years old. He was buried on January 25, 1980 at Silverbrook Cemetery in Niles, Michigan.

Loring, Susan Eileen (1950-2009) Sue was born Susan Reed on March 27, 1950 in Niles, Michigan. She was adopted by Francis and B. Carolyn (Kloko) Pfauth. She grew up in Michigan as the eldest of two siblings. Sue married Kenneth Polmanteer. They divorced, having no children. She was remarried to Charles Loring. They had three children. They were divorced. She was a bus driver for public schools. Sue passed away from Septic Shock due to Necrotizing Fasciitis-Perineum on February 28, 2009 in Kalamazoo, Michigan. She was 58 years old. She was cremated.

McDonald, Doris Arlene (1931-1995) Doris was born Doris Kloko on November 9, 1931 in Porter, Indiana. She grew up in Michigan, being the fifth child of six siblings. Doris was married on October 23, 1948 to William Reed in Niles, Michigan. They had two children. They were divorced. She was remarried on January 24, 1951 to Arden F Lancaster in Howe, Indiana. They had one child. They divorced. She was also remarried to Alvin H Smith. They had four children. They were divorced. She was remarried once again to Gordon McDonald. They had no children. Doris passed away from Cancer of the Lung with Metastasis to Adrenal Gland and Left Axilla on November 16, 1995 in Watervliet, Michigan. She was 64 years old. She was buried on November 18, 1995 at Fairview Memorial Cemetery in Watervliet, Michigan.

Mann, Myrtle Alice (1884-1951) Myrtle was born Myrtle Cross on May 9, 1884. She grew up in Michigan, the youngest of five siblings. Myrtle married Allan L DuBreuil. They had one child. Myrtle became widowed on June 6, 1917. She remarried Clyde D Mann, having no children. Myrtle passed away from Uremia due to Arteriosclerosis Generalized due to Hypertension, Chronic Nephritis and Left Hemiplegia on July 24, 1951 in Watervliet, Michigan. She was 67 years old. She was buried on July 26, 1951 at Coloma Cemetery in Coloma, Michigan.

Pfauth, Beulah Carolyn (1924-1986) Carolyn was born Beulah Kloko on November 17, 1924. She grew up in Michigan, being the third child of six siblings. Carolyn married Francis Pfauth in Oceanside, California. They adopted two children. Carolyn passed away on April 21, 1986 in Watervliet, Michigan. She was 61 years old. She was buried on April 24, 1986 at Coloma Cemetery in Coloma, Michigan.

Reed, Ezra Henry (1860-1936) Ezra was born in January 11, 1860. He grew up in Indiana, being the third child of six siblings. Ezra was married in 1887 to Sarah Harter in Indiana. They had nine children. Ezra passed away on February 14, 1936. He was 76 years old. He was buried on March 5, 1936 at Silverbrook Cemetery in Niles, Michigan.

Reed, Josephine Esther (1906-1998) Josie was born Josephine Leggett on October 27, 1906. She grew up in Michigan, being the second child of six siblings. Josie was married on February 9, 1924 to William Reed in St. Joseph, Michigan. They had three children. Josie passed away on November 23, 1998 in Fort Myers, Florida. She was 92 years old. She was buried on December 1, 1998 at Silverbrook Cemetery in Niles, Michigan.

Reed, May (1905-1918) May was born on March 17, 1905. She grew up in Indiana, being the eighth child of nine siblings. May passed away from Pnuemonia Broncho due to Influenza on November 9, 1918 in Niles, Michigan. She was 13 years old. She was buried on November 12, 1918 at Silverbrook Cemetery in Niles, Michigan.

Reed, Sarah Elizabeth (1866-1927) Sarah was born Sarah Harter on April 3, 1866. She grew up in Indiana. Sarah was married in 1887 to Ezra Reed in Indiana. They had nine children. Sarah passed away from Valvular Heart Disease on July 31, 1927 in Niles, Michigan. She was 61 years old. She was buried at Silverbrook Cemetery in Niles, Michigan.

Reed, William (1897-1976) William was born on January 2, 1897 in Indiana. He grew up in Indiana, being the fourth child of nine siblings. William married Pearl. They had three children. They were divorced. He was remarried on February 9, 1924 to Josephine Leggett in St. Joseph, Michigan. They had three children. William worked on the railroad. He was also a mechanic and garage owner. William passed away on September 22, 1976 in Fort Myers, Florida. He was 79 years old. He was buried on September 24, 1976 at Silverbrook Cemetery in Niles, Michigan.

Reed, William (1926-1951) William was born on October 28, 1926 in Niles, Michigan. He grew up in Michigan, being the fourth child of six siblings. William was married on October 23, 1948 to Doris Kloko in Niles, Michigan. They had two children. They were divorced. William was a truck driver. He also served in the U.S. Navy. William passed away from a Basil Skull Fracture due to Motorcycle Accident on July 29, 1951 in Niles, Michigan. He was 24 years old. He was buried on August 1, 1951 at Silverbrook Cemetery in Niles, Michigan.

Reinke, Augusta Henrietta (1849-1937) Augusta was born Augusta Able on September 16, 1849 in Germany. She grew up in Germany. Augusta married Julius Reinke. They had five children. Augusta passed away on September 25, 1937 in Dayton, Michigan. She was 88 years old. She was buried at Oak Ridge Cemetery in Buchanan, Michigan.

Reinke, Caroline (1818-1911) Caroline was born Caroline Lipke on April 15, 1818 in Germany. She was married in 1834 to Jacob Godfrey Reinke in Germany. They had ten children. Caroline passed away from Acute Bronchitis due to Senile Debility on January 26, 1911. She was 82 years old. She was buried on January 29, 1911 at Bakertown Cemetery in Buchanan, Michigan.

Reinke, Julius (1848-1934) Julius was born on April 30, 1848 in Posen, Germany. He grew up in Germany, being the seventh child of ten siblings. Julius married Augusta Able. They had five children. He also declared his Intention for Naturalization on March 30, 1888 in Buchanan, Michigan. Julius passed away on March 3, 1934 in Bertrand, Michigan. He was 85 years old. He was buried at Oak Ridge Cemetery in Buchanan, Michigan.

Seas, John (1807-1880) John was born on October 25, 1807 in Pennsylvania. He married Lydia Haberling. They had five children. He was a farmer. John passed away from Disease of Liver on October 25, 1880. He was 73 years old. He was buried at Beard Cemetery in Leonidas, Michigan.

Seas, Lena (1893-1951) Lena was born in 1893. Lena passed away in 1951. She was about 58 years old. She was buried at Beard Cemetery in Leonidas, Michigan.

Seas, Lydia (1812-1892) Lydia was born Lydia Haberling on August 10, 1812 in Pennsylvania. She married John Seas. They had five children. Lydia passed away from Disentary on October 10, 1892. She was 80 years old. She was buried at Beard Cemetery in Leonidas, Michigan.

Seas, Peter (1843-1920) Peter was born in 1843 in Pennsylvania. He was the middle child of five siblings. Peter married Mary. He was a carpenter. Peter passed away in 1920. He was about 57 years old. He was buried at Beard Cemetery in Leonidas, Michigan.

Seas, William H (1846-1926) William was born in 1846 in Pennsylvania. He was the second child of five siblings. He was a shoemaker. William passed away in 1926. He was about 80 years old. He was buried at Beard Cemetery in Leonidas, Michigan.

Shisley, Bernice (1902-1957) Bernice was born Bernice Bowersox on January 7, 1902 in Three Rivers, Michigan. She grew up in Michigan, being the second child of six siblings. Bernice married Ervin Kloko. They had seven children. She became widowed on April 3, 1849. She remarried F S Shisley. They had no children. Bernice passed away from Cerebral Embalism due to Grade IV Rheumatic due to Heart Disease on June 8, 1957 in Sturgis, Michigan. She was 55 years old. She was buried on June 10, 1957 at Silverbrook Cemetery in Niles, Michigan.

Sieczkowski, Martha (1899-1972) Martha was born Martha Szczesniak on July 21, 1899 in Chicago, Illinois. She grew up in South Chicago, being the middle child of seven siblings. Martha married Walter Sieczkowski. They had children. Martha passed away in October of 1972. She was 73 years old. She was buried on October 14, 1972 at Holy Cross Cemetery in Calumet City, Illinois.

Swails, Mary (1859-?) Mary was born Mary Cross about 1859. She grew up in Michigan, being the youngest of six siblings. mary was married on September 3, 1872 to Edward H Swails. They had eight children.

Szczesniak, Casimer (1907-1974) Casimer was born on July 17, 1907 in Chicago, Illinois. He grew up in South Chicago, being the youngest of seven siblings. Casimer married Sylvia. They had no children. He became widowed in 1964. He remarried, having no children. Casimer passed away in December of 1974. He was 67 years old. He was buried on December 24, 1974 at Holy Cross Cemetery in Calumet City, Illinois.

Szczesniak, Malgorzata (1873-1930) Malgorzata was born Malgorzata Dominiak about 1873 in Szubin, Poland. Malgorzata was married on November 15, 1892 to Wojciech Szczesniak at the St Michael's Church in Chicago, Illinois. They had seven children. Malgorzata passed away from Carcinoma of Uterus on July 4, 1930 in Chicago, Illinois. She was about 57 years old. She was buried on July 8, 1930 at Holy Cross Cemetery in Calumet City, Illinois.

Szczesniak, Walter (1893-1964) Walter was born in 1893 in Chicago, Illinois. He grew up in South Chicago, being the eldest of seven siblings. Walter married Bertha. They had children. Walter passed away in 1964. He was about 71 years old. He was buried on June 3, 1964 at Holy Cross Cemetery in Calumet City, Illinois.

Szczesniak, Wojciech (1871-1947) Wojciech was born Adalbert Szczesniak about 1871 in Poland. Wojciech was married on November 15, 1892 to Malgorzata Dominiak at the St Michael's Church in Chicago, Illinois. They had seven children. Wojciech passed away from Acute Monocystic Leukemia on May 25, 1947. He was about 75 years old. He was buried on May 29, 1947 at Holy Cross Cemetery in Calumet City, Illinois.

Waldron, Karen Lorain (1951-1993) Karen was born Karen Kloko on October 10, 1951 in Niles, Michigan. She grew up in Michigan, being the second child of four siblings. Karen married Rick Waldron. They had no children. She was a medical transcriptionist. Karen passed away on October 21, 1993 in Niles, Michigan. She was 42 years old. She was buried on October 25, 1993 at Mission Hills Memorial Gardens in Niles, Michigan.

Other Books by David Holmer:

"Eat Yourself Thin"
"I Like Veggies!"
"I Like to Walk!"
"Who Are You?"

www.DavidHolmer.com

Would you like to see your manuscript become a book?

If you are interested in becoming a PublishAmerica author, please submit your manuscript for possible publication to us at:

acquisitions@publishamerica.com

You may also mail in your manuscript to:

**PublishAmerica
PO Box 151
Frederick, MD 21705**

www.publishamerica.com

CPSIA information can be obtained at www.ICGtesting.com
Printed in the USA
236016LV00002B/101/P